THE
COMPLETE
GREEK
COOKBOOK

2 Books In 1: 120 Recipes For
Traditional Food From Greece

Emma Yang

Adele Tyler

GREEK

COOKBOOK

60 Recipes for Classic Food from
Greece

Emma Yang

CONTENTS

INTRODUCTION 12

CHAPTER 1: CLASSIC AND FAMOUS GREEK DISHES 16

FAMOUS GREEK RIBS 17

LAMB KLEFTIKO 18

THE ULTIMATE GREEK MEZE PLATTER 20

GREEK SHRIMP WITH TOMATOES & FETA 21

GREEK GREEN BEANS 22

RABBIT MEAT WITH CRETAN PASTA 23

PRAWN SAGANAKI 24

CHICKEN IN RETSINA WINE.. 26

HOME-STYLE GREEK SANDWICHES 27

LEMON SPAHETTI... 28

RAGU TAGLIATELLE 30

MISISSIPI POT ROAST 31

GREEK SEA BASS.. 32

GREEK LAMB ROAST.. 34

GREEK SPETSIOTIKO FISH 35

GREEK CHICKEN KEBABS 36

GREEK-STYLE SLOW COOKED LAMB SHANKS........................ 38

SHEET PAN CHICKEN AND VEGETABLES 39

GREEK LAMB CHOPS 40

GREEK STUFFED SQUID 42

GREEK GRAVOS WITH PEPPERS 44

CUTTLEFISH WITH SPINACH..45

GREEK BEEF STEW 46

GREEK OCTUPUS WITH EGGPLANTS 47

GREEK ZUCCHINI FRITTERS 48

GREEK COD WITH GARLIC SAUCE...............................50

GREEK CHEESE PIES 51

GREEK RICE WITH FISH..52

GREEK BEEF AND ORZO STEW 53

GREEK SPINACH PIE...54

CHAPTER 2: MACEDONIAN RECIPES 57

FRIED PASTRY WITH SYRUP...58

LAMB INTESTINES EASTER DELICACY 60

STUFFED LAMB'S STOMACH...61

TAVCE GRAVCE..64

POTATO STEW 66

CHAPTER 3: RECIPES FROM CYPRUS..................... 68

SAGANAKI FRIED HALLOUMI CHEESE 69

ZUCCHINI SCRAMBLED EGGS WITH HALLOUMI 70

KOUPES ROLLS FROM CYPRUS......................................72

CYPRUS ARMY PORK CHOPS.. 73

CYPRIOT STYLE FRIES 74

TRADITIONAL TOASTED CYPRUS SANDWICH 76

CHAPTER 4: CRETAN RECIPES.................................. 78

CRETAN DAKOS.. 79

BRAISED CRETAN LAMB 80

CRETAN CUCUMBER & TOMATO SALAD 82

CRETAN VILLAGE SALAD.. 84

CRETAN EGGS WITH WILD WEEDS... 85

CRETAN CHEESE MEZE WITH SUN DRIED TOMATOES 86

CHAPTER 5: AEGEAN ISLANDS RECIPES............................. 88

ISLAND OMELET... 89

ISLAND SALAD WITH CHICKENA & AVOCADO...................................... 90

ISLANDS QUINOA SALAD.. 92

ISLANDS GRILLED BREAD AND TOMATOES... 93

ISLAND SHRIMP WITH PASTA 94

SHRIMP RECIPE WITH TOMATO AND FETA 96

CHAPTER 6: RECIPES FROM IONIAN ISLANDS.................. 98

POLENTA.. 99

SKORDOSTOUMBI.. 100

CORFU DELICIOUS BIANCO... 102

NOSTIMO FAGITO 103

FRIED ANCHOVIES..104

MACARONI CHEESE..106

CONCLUSION 107

INTRODUCTION 110

CHAPTER 1: CLASSIC AND FAMOUS GREEK DISHES ... 113

SKORDALIA 114

GREEK HONEY COOKIES..116

GREEK BAKED ORZO 117

GREEK WALNUT CAKE 118

GREK MEATBALLS...120

STUFFED GRAPE LEAVES...121

MOUSSAKA 122

GREK STUFFED PEPPERS 124

GREEK BEAN SOUP (FESOLADA)..125

GREEK PITA BREAD 126

GREEK GREEN BEANS..128

GREEK SALAD 129

GREEK FETA DIP..130

CHICKEN SOUVLAKI...131

GREEK BAKLAVA...132

GREEK CHICKPEA SOUP..134

TIROPITA...135

GREEK EGGPLANT DIP 136

GREEK ORANGE CAKE... 137

GREEK LENTIL SOUP... 138

FASOLATHA 140

LOUKOUMADES 141

GREEK LEMON POTATOES.. 142

GREEK LEMON CHICKEN SOUP 143

CHICKEN GYROS... 144

TZATZIKI.. 146

SPANOKOPITA.. 148

GREEK FRIED CHEESE... 149

GREEK FRIES.. 150

CHAPTER 2: MACEDONIAN RECIPES................................. 152

MACEDONIAN FISH WITH RICE 153

MACEDONIAN KEBABS... 154

MACEDONIAN TERRATOR... 156

MACEDONIAN STYLE JUICY MEATBALLS 158

MACEDONIAN MACARONI 159

MACEDONIAN EGGPLANT SALAD 160

CHAPTER 3: RECIPES FROM CYPRUS................................. 163

BEEF STIFADO 164

COUPES 166

CYPRUS GYRO BURGER 167

CYPRIOT PASTITIO 168

CYPRIOT TALATOURI TZATZIKI... 170

CYPRIOT RICE AND LEMON STEW WITH SPINACH 171

CHAPTER 4: CRETAN RECIPES... 173

CRETAN MEAT PIE... 174

CRETAN WEDDING RISOTTO... 175

BOUREKI 176

CRETAN POTATOES.. 178

CRETAN TOMATO SALAD 179

CRETAN CHEESE PIE WITH THYME AND HONEY 180

CHAPTER 5: AEGEAN ISLANDS RECIPES 182

ISLAND TAVERNA'S LAMB CHOPS... 183

GRILLED OCTUPUS WITH LEMON, OREGANO AND OLIVE OIL......... 184

ISLANDS STEAK SALAD.. 186

AEGAN TOMATO SAUCE SPAGHETTI.. 187

ISLANDS CHICKEN SHISH KEBABS.. 188

PASTELI-SESAME-HONEY CONFECTION 190

CHAPTER 6: IONIAN ISLANDS RECIPES............................. 192

FRIGANIA... 193

ORANGE-CURRANT SCONES.. 194

TUNISIAN TOMATO SOUP WITH CHICKPEA 196

TSIGARELI.. 197

RABBIT STEWED IN TOMATO AND RED WINE........................ 198

ISLAND SOFRITO 199

CONCLUSION 200

Introduction

Greece, located in the southern region of Europe, has a rich culture and history that can still be found across the country. One of the most important things of their culture is its distinct food, which has enticed both visitors and residents for many years. You'll learn all you need to know about the interesting food and preparation methods of Greek food right here.

The ancient Greeks ate three meals a day on average. Breakfast was the first food of the day, followed by a mid-day meal and an early dinner. Breakfast comprised a few light items, such as bread soaked in wine and sometimes accompanied by olives or figs. The mid-day supper was a quick gathering that featured modest yet tasty prepared meals. The most significant meal of the day was the evening supper. The dishes were made with a range of ingredients, including beans, legumes, wheat, seafood, various meats, and vegetables. Many of these are still in use nowadays, improving over time while maintaining their original and historical appeal.

Even though Greek cuisine has developed significantly throughout the country's history, many classic dishes are still served today. The "Mediterranean Triad" comprises the characteristic Greek food, which was evolved from a broad Mediterranean taste. Grain, olive oil, and alcohol are all included in this category. The cornerstones of Greek food include the olives, olive oil as mentioned above, grain and berries, plants, sweets, and fish. Lamb is commonly utilized as well. Greece has one of the healthier diets on the planet.

In addition to olive oil, spices are a common element in Greek cuisine. Greece's residents like to season their food with a variety of spices. Because most spices are cultivated locally, they are plentiful in many areas. Mint, cilantro, coriander, spice, paprika, rosemary, and saffron are the most popular. Coriander, commonly known as parsley, is used in various cuisines, from beef and pork marinades to hummus. Among the most famous spices, basil is frequently used in marinades and salads. For thousands of years, these seasonings have been a mainstay of Greek cuisine, and they will most likely continue to be so for hundreds more.

Throughout Greek history, it has not changed. The Greeks' usage of fingers while eating is one of the few traditions that has faded away with time, but not completely. Utensils were rarely utilized in ancient times. Almost all of the typical dishes were eaten with one's fingers. While a few items are still served this way, most are served with a knife and fork. The similarities between now and then are much too numerous to mention. The subtleties of Greek food, like the nation of Greece itself, have stood the test of time. Olive oil, for example, is used in practically every meal and is a source of pride for the residents, who are famed for producing their olive oil from local olives. Olive oil has become a basic requirement for most people throughout history, not just in food but also in wine.

There are probably hundreds of delicious Greek foods to select from, but a few favorites stand out. Soup is among the few dishes in which several of the most common components may be included in the recipe. The Fassolatha, a rich white beans soup, and the Avgolemono, a creamy noodle soup, are two of the most popular soups among Greeks. Saganaki, which is essentially just grilled cheese with a Greek touch, and Moussaka and Baklava, are some of the most popular meals in Greece. Moussaka is a typical Greek stew made with eggplant and seasoned pork, and Baklava is a delectable Greek confection that has enchanted tourists for ages. Not only these recipes but many other recipes are famous from Greek cuisine. Try these recipes and add some Greek flavors in your food.

Chapter 1: Classic and Famous Greek Dishes

The importance of food in Greek culture cannot be overestimated. The social act of sharing food is more important than the dish itself. Fruits and vegetables, grains, beans and lentils, fish, and certain dairy products like cheeses and yogurt make up the typical Greek diet. Because Greece is abundant in fruits and veggies, and many Greeks work in or near agriculture, they use raw, fresh ingredients and vegetables. Greek and Mediterranean diets are recognized as among the healthiest in the world, in addition to the Greek proclivity for smothering everything with olive oil. Whatever holiday you celebrate in Greece, there is a wide variety of holiday cuisine to delight any palate. Here I have included some classic and delectable recipes from Greek cuisine.

FAMOUS GREEK RIBS

INGREDIENTS

- **Glaze**
- 1 teaspoon fresh oregano
- 1 teaspoon fresh thyme
- 1 garlic clove
- ½ small red onion
- 1 tablespoon red wine vinegar
- 1 tablespoon honey
- **Rub**
- 2 racks pork ribs
- Juice of 1 lemon
- Pinch kosher salt
- 1 tablespoon oregano
- 2 teaspoons paprika
- 2 teaspoons coriander seed
- 1 tablespoon garlic salt
- **Finish**
- 1 tablespoon olive oil
- Drizzle of honey
- Sea salt
- 1 tablespoon oregano
- 1 lemon

COOK TIME: 3 hours
SERVING: 4q

INSTRUCTIONS

1. Put all components in a mixing bowl to make the rub.
2. Use lemon juice to moisten the ribs before applying the rub to both sides.
3. Make sure the grill is set up for indirect heat.
4. Wrap the ribs in foil and cook for 60 minutes on the cold side of the grill.
5. Meanwhile, combine all glaze ingredients in a mixing bowl.
6. Put one third of the glaze on top of the ribs after 60 minutes.
7. Return the ribs to the grill and cook for half an hour with the meat side down.
8. Transfer the ribs from the grill after 60 minutes of cooking and let them rest in foil for half an hour.
9. Raise the heat on the grill to medium-high.
10. Half the lemon and cook the flesh side down.
11. Heat for another 2 - 3 minutes on the other side.
12. If desired, remove the ribs from the grill and season with oregano, sea salt, lemon, olive oil, and honey.

LAMB KLEFTIKO

INGREDIENTS

- ½ ripe tomato
- Salt and pepper
- 200g kefalotyri cheese
- 5 potatoes
- ½ cup olive oil
- ½ cup dry white wine
- Juice of half a lemon
- 1 tablespoon dried oregano
- 4 cloves of garlic
- 2 tablespoons mustard
- 2 small red onions
- 3 bell peppers
- 1.2 kg leg of lamb

COOK TIME: 4 hours
SERVING: 6

INSTRUCTIONS

1. Pour the white wine, olive oil, and lemon juice over the veggies in the bowl with the lamb pieces.
2. Season with salt and pepper after adding the garlic, mustard, and oregano.
3. Use your hands to combine all of the ingredients.
4. Marinate the lamb for three hours in the mixture.
5. Blend in the cheese in the same bowl.
6. Preheat the oven to 175 degrees Celsius.
7. Sprinkle the potatoes with salt and a bit of oregano and place them in the center of the parchment paper.
8. Pour the lamb marinade over the potatoes and arrange the lamb and veggies on top of it.
9. Layer the sliced tomato on the lamb kleftiko and fold it into a pouch.
10. In a preheated oven, roast the lamb kleftiko for about 1 hour 45 minutes, or until soft.
11. Remove the lamb kleftiko from the oven.
12. Return the lamb to the oven for another 20 minutes or until browned, rubbing it with the marinade again.
13. Garnish the lamb kleftiko with a spoonful of yogurt on top. Enjoy!

THE ULTIMATE GREEK MEZE PLATTER

INGREDIENTS

- 1 cup Easy Greek Tzatziki
- 1 cup hummus
- **Add-Ins**
- Fresh tomatoes
- Warmed pita bread
- Feta cheese
- Baby cucumbers
- Dolmades
- Kalamata olives
- Greek meatballs with feta cheese

COOK TIME: 60 mins
SERVING: 6

INSTRUCTIONS

1. To make serving easy, arrange all items on a big dish.
2. Drizzle olive oil over the feta cheese and season with dry oregano.
3. Drizzle some olive oil on top of the hummus and sprinkle some toasted pine nuts on top.
4. Serve with hot pita bread.

GREEK SHRIMP WITH TOMATOES & FETA

INGREDIENTS

- 56 g feta cheese
- 6 Kalamata olives
- Chopped mint leaves
- Chopped parsley leaves
- 737.088 g canned tomato
- Juice of ½ lemon
- Greek olive oil
- 1 large red onion
- Pinch red pepper flakes
- 6 garlic cloves
- 1 ½ teaspoon oregano
- 1 ½ teaspoon dill weed
- Kosher salt
- Black pepper
- 1 ½ lb. large shrimp

COOK TIME: 30 mins
SERVING: 6

INSTRUCTIONS

1. Place the shrimp in a large mixing bowl after patting them dry.
2. Season with red pepper flakes, dill weed, dried oregano, pepper, kosher salt, and chopped garlic.
3. Toss with extra virgin olive oil until well combined.
4. Heat two tablespoons of olive oil in a big heavy pan over medium heat, combine the onion and garlic in a mixing bowl.
5. Season with salt and pepper after adding the tomatoes and lemon juice.
6. Bring to a boil, then reduce to low heat and allow it to simmer for fifteen minutes.
7. Add the shrimp that have been marinated.
8. Cook for approximately 5–7 minutes.
9. In a separate bowl, combine the fresh mint and parsley leaves.
10. Finish with feta cheese and black olives.
11. Serve on a bed of plain orzo.

Tip: The essential thing to remember here is not overcooked the shrimp.

GREEK GREEN BEANS

INGREDIENTS

- 2 teaspoons sugar
- Salt to taste
- 2 pounds green beans
- 3 large tomatoes
- 2 cups chopped onions
- 1 clove garlic
- ¾ cup olive oil

COOK TIME: 75 mins
SERVING: 8

INSTRUCTIONS

1. In a large frying pan, heat the oil over moderate flame.
2. In a pan, cook and sauté the onions and garlic until soft.
3. Combine the sugar, tomatoes, green beans, and salt in a pan.
4. Reduce to low heat and simmer for another 45 minutes, or until the beans are tender.
5. Serve with yogurt.

RABBIT MEAT WITH CRETAN PASTA

INGREDIENTS

- Salt, pepper, oregano
- 1 package maggiri egg noodles
- 1 tomato
- 1 lemon
- Extra virgin olive oil
- 1 white glass of wine
- 2 onions
- 1 rabbit (large pieces)

COOK TIME: 50 mins
SERVING: 4

INSTRUCTIONS

1. Wash the rabbit parts thoroughly and add salt and pepper.
2. Drizzle some olive oil in a heated pan and sauté the rabbit.
3. Add the wine after both sides have been cooked.
4. Combine the onions, tomato, and water in a mixing bowl.
5. When the water begins to boil, reduce the heat, add the lemon juice, and season with oregano.
6. Allow it to boil for a few minutes before removing it from the heat.
7. Cook the Maggiri noodles for 3-4 minutes in salted water, then sieve and drizzle with olive oil.
8. In a deep platter, combine the noodles, rabbit, and sauce. Serve hot.

PRAWN SAGANAKI

INGREDIENTS

- Chopped parsley (garnish)
- Salt and pepper
- 450 g raw jumbo prawns
- 200 g feta cheese
- 400 g diced tomatoes
- 120 ml white wine
- 2 bay leaves
- 240 g tomatoes
- ¼ teaspoon chili flakes
- 2 tablespoons tomato paste
- 1 teaspoon dried thyme
- ½ teaspoon salt
- 3 garlic cloves
- 1 teaspoon sugar
- 1 large onion
- 2 tablespoons olive oil

COOK TIME: 55 mins
SERVING: 6

INSTRUCTIONS

1. Heat the oil in a big oven-safe baking dish. Sauté the onion for 5 minutes on moderate flame.
2. Cook for a few minutes after adding the chill flakes, thyme, sugar, salt, garlic, and bay leaves.
3. Bring the tomato paste, tomatoes, passata, and wine to a low boil.
4. Cook for 20-30 minutes, stirring periodically.
5. Add the prawns and toss them around in the sauce until they become pink.
6. Heat on a hot grill with crumbled feta on top.
7. Check the spice and season to taste with salt and pepper.
8. With enough crusty bread, serve.

CHICKEN IN RETSINA WINE

INGREDIENTS

- 1 cup retsina
- Salt and pepper to season
- 3 bay leaves
- Juice of 1 lemon
- 1 teaspoon coriander seeds
- 10 green olives
- 6 garlic cloves
- 3 sprigs rosemary
- ½ cup olive oil
- 3 onions
- 4 chicken thighs

COOK TIME: 35 mins
SERVING: 4

INSTRUCTIONS

1. Season the chicken using salt and pepper.
2. Heat the olive oil in a skillet and cook the chicken for about 7 minutes, or until lightly browned on all sides.
3. Cook for another 5 minutes after adding the coriander seeds, garlic, and onion.
4. Combine the retsina and lime juice in a skillet.
5. To deglaze the pan, stir the mixture.
6. Next, add the olives, bay leaves, and rosemary.
7. Simmer for fifteen minutes, or until the vegetables are soft.
8. Serve the chicken with simple rice and a salad as a side dish.

HOME-STYLE GREEK SANDWICHES

INGREDIENTS

- 1 cup feta
- 6 Ladopsomo pieces of bread
- 1 cup mustard greens
- ½ small red onion
- 4 radishes
- 2 plum tomatoes
- 12 pitted kalamata olives
- 6 pickled peperoncini
- ½ teaspoon oregano
- 1 small Kirby cucumber
- Salt and black pepper
- 2 tablespoons olive oil
- 2 tablespoons dill
- 3 tablespoons red wine vinegar
- 2 roasted red peppers
- 2 garlic cloves
- ½ cup Greek yogurt
- 1 medium cucumber

COOK TIME: *5 hours*
SERVING: *6*

INSTRUCTIONS

1. Pulse the cucumber in a stick blender until it is minced.
2. Place on a kitchen towel to absorb any excess liquid.
3. Combine the dill, garlic, roasted peppers, yogurt, and vinegar in a food processor and pulse until smooth.
4. Toss the drained cucumber with the yogurt mixture and whisk thoroughly.
5. Add salt and pepper in the tzatziki to taste.
6. Combine olive oil and oregano in a large mixing dish.
7. Toss together the onion, mustard greens, tomatoes, radishes, pepperoncini, olives, cucumber, and feta.
8. Add salt & pepper to taste.
9. Top each piece of bread with tzatziki and the salad. Serve immediately.

LEMON SPAHETTI

INGREDIENTS

- 1 tablespoon lemon zest
- 1/3 cup basil leaves
- ½ cup lemon juice
- Salt and black pepper
- 2/3 cup olive oil
- 2/3 cup Parmesan
- 1 pound spaghetti

COOK TIME: 18 mins
SERVING: 6

INSTRUCTIONS

1. Add the pasta in a large pot of hot, salted water for about 10 minutes, or until cooked but still firm to the biting.
2. Combine the parmesan, oil, and lemon juice in a large mixing bowl.
3. Save one cup of the cooking liquid after draining the pasta.
4. Toss the pasta with the lemon sauce and the cooking liquid that has been set aside.
5. Add salt & pepper to taste. Serve immediately.

Tip: Lemon zest and basil leaves are optional garnishes.

RAGU TAGLIATELLE

INGREDIENTS

- Black pepper to taste
- 400g of fresh tagliatelle
- 400g diced tomatoes
- Salt to taste
- 300g minced beef
- 35ml red wine
- 1 large carrot
- 1-2 celery stalks
- 1 small onion
- 1 cloves garlic
- 2 tablespoons olive oil

COOK TIME: 60 mins
SERVING: 4

INSTRUCTIONS

1. In a cooking pot, heat the olive oil over moderate flame.
2. Cook until the chopped onions are tender.
3. After that, sauté the garlic cloves, celery, carrots, beef mince, red wine, and tomatoes.
4. Add salt & pepper to taste.
5. Cover and cook for half an hour on low to moderate heat until the sauce is thickened.
6. Cook the tagliatelle for at least 3-4 minutes in a big saucepan of well-salted boiling water.
7. Toss the tagliatelle with the bolognese sauce.
8. Sprinkle finely grated Parmigiano Reggiano generously on top.

MISISSIPI POT ROAST

INGREDIENTS

- 1 package ranch dressing
- Salt and black pepper
- ½ jar pepperoncini juice
- 1 packet au jus gravy mix
- ½ jar pepperoncini
- 1 (3 pounds) chuck roast

COOK TIME: 8 hours
SERVING: 8

INSTRUCTIONS

1. In a slow cooker, whisk together salt, buttermilk ranch dressing, au jus mix, pepperoncini, chuck roast, pepperoncini juice, and pepper.
2. Cook on low heat for 8 hours or until the roast is fork-tender.
3. With two forks, pull the chuck apart.
4. To keep it warm, cover it with aluminum foil.
5. Serve with your favorite sauce.

GREEK SEA BASS

INGREDIENTS

- Salt and pepper
- Lemon zest for garnish
- ½ bunch parsley
- 1 tablespoon olive oil
- 2 cloves of garlic
- 150ml white wine
- 15 kalamata olives
- 15 capers
- 1 fennel bulb
- 1 tomato
- 1 lemon
- 2 whole sea bass

COOK TIME: 30 mins
SERVING: 4

INSTRUCTIONS

1. Preheat the oven to 180 degrees Fahrenheit and place the sea bass on a baking pan.
2. Stuff fennel, lemon, olives, tomato, and capers into the cavity of each fish.
3. Sprinkle with salt and freshly ground pepper after adding the white wine.
4. Drizzle olive oil over the sea bass and top with chopped parsley.
5. Preheat the oven to 190°C and bake the filled sea bass for 20-25 minutes.
6. Remove the baking pan from the oven and set it aside to cool for 3-4 minutes before gently unwrapping it.
7. Garnish it with lemon zest.

GREEK LAMB ROAST

INGREDIENTS

- 400g can tomato
- Large handful of kalamata olives
- 6 tablespoons olive oil
- 1 ½kg new potatoes
- 1 bunch oregano
- Zest and juice 1 lemon
- 6 garlic cloves
- 1 large leg of lamb

COOK TIME: 1.5 hours
SERVING: 8

INSTRUCTION

1. Preheat the oven to 240 degrees Celsius.
2. In a pestle and mortar, pound the lemon zest, oregano, garlic, and a bit of salt, then add the lemon juice and a splash of olive oil.
3. Using a sharp knife, make cuts on the lamb all over, then stuff as much herb mixture as you can into the openings.
4. Combine the potatoes, olive oil, and herb paste in a mixing bowl.
5. Place the lamb in the middle of the potatoes and cook for twenty minutes.
6. For medium-rare, roast for 1 hour 15 minutes.
7. Place the roasting tin over a moderate flame, then add the canned tomatoes and olives to the pan contents and cook for a few minutes.
8. Garnish the lamb with a side salad and potatoes and sauce.

GREEK SPETSIOTIKO FISH

INGREDIENTS

- ¾ cup plain bread crumbs
- ¼ cup Greek olive oil
- ½ cup dry white wine
- Salt and pepper to taste
- 3 garlic cloves
- ½ cup fresh parsley
- 1 ½ cups fresh tomatoes
- 2 ½ pounds fish fillets

COOK TIME: 60 mins
SERVING: 4

INSTRUCTIONS

1. Season the fish lightly with salt and keep it chilled for half an hour.
2. Mix the parsley, garlic, tomatoes, and wine in a large bowl and set aside half an hour.
3. Preheat oven to 375 degrees Fahrenheit.
4. Sprinkle the fish with a bit more salt and pepper if desired.
5. Place in a baking dish that has been gently greased.
6. Serve the fish with the marinade and breadcrumbs on top.
7. Drizzle with extra virgin olive oil.
8. Preheat oven to 200°F and bake for 20–25 minutes.
9. Remove the pan from the oven and serve.

GREEK CHICKEN KEBABS

INGREDIENTS

- 12 chicken thighs
- **For the Marinade**
- 4 tablespoons olive oil
- Small bunch parsley
- 1 tablespoon dried oregano
- 2 teaspoons paprika
- 1 teaspoon ground cinnamon
- 1 teaspoon ground allspice
- Zest and juice of 1 lemon
- 2 garlic cloves

COOK TIME: 55 mins
SERVING: 4

INSTRUCTIONS

1. Combine all of the marinade ingredients in a large mixing bowl.
2. Combine the chicken thighs with the marinade and stir to combine.
3. Lit a lidded barbeque.
4. Thread the chicken pieces onto two metal skewers.
5. Place the chicken kebab on the side of metal skewers.
6. Cook for 45-55 minutes with the lid down.
7. Before slicing, cover the chicken with foil and let it rest for twenty minutes.
8. Slice the kebab chicken into strips and insert them inside pitas that have been reheated on the grill.
9. Serve cucumber salad, red onion, tomato, dill yogurt sauce, and crisp lettuce on the side.

GREEK-STYLE SLOW COOKED LAMB SHANKS

INGREDIENTS

- 1 red pepper
- 100ml white wine
- 2 tablespoons olive oil
- 1 ½kg waxy potatoes
- 3 bay leaves
- 1 large lemon
- 2 teaspoons dried oregano
- Large pinch of cinnamon
- 1 teaspoon dried rosemary
- 1 teaspoon dried thyme
- 4 garlic cloves
- 4 lamb shanks

COOK TIME: 3 hours
SERVING: 6

INSTRUCTIONS

1. Combine the lamb shanks, lime juice, bay leaves, cinnamon, dried oregano, thyme, rosemary, garlic, and olive oil in a large mixing bowl.
2. Season to taste, then combine everything in a large mixing bowl.
3. Preheat the oven to 200 degrees Celsius.
4. Place the potatoes and peppers in a big roasting pan and pour the wine over them.
5. Remove the lamb from the marinade and set it aside; pour the remaining marinade over the vegetables.
6. Toss everything together, then place the lamb on top of the vegetables.
7. Bake for two and a half hours, carefully covered with foil.
8. If the tin appears to be dry, drizzle in additional oil.
9. Cover and bake for another half an hour.
10. Allow 5 minutes of resting time before scattering the feta and fresh oregano on top.

SHEET PAN CHICKEN AND VEGETABLES

INGREDIENTS

- 6 chicken thighs
- 6 cups baby spinach
- ¾ teaspoon pepper
- ½ teaspoon paprika
- ¼ teaspoon salt
- 1 teaspoon dried rosemary
- 2 tablespoons olive oil
- 3 garlic cloves
- 1 large onion
- 2 pounds red potatoes

COOK TIME: 45 mins
SERVING: 6

INSTRUCTIONS

1. Preheat the oven to 415 degrees Fahrenheit.
2. Toss rosemary, salt, potatoes, garlic, oil, onion, and pepper in a large mixing bowl to coat.
3. Place in a baking pan that has been sprayed with cooking spray.
4. Combine paprika, the leftover rosemary, salt, and pepper in a mixing bowl.
5. Toss the chicken with the paprika mixture and place it on the veggies.
6. Allow cooking for 35-40 minutes till veggies are just soft.
7. Transfer the chicken to a serving plate and set it aside to keep warm.
8. Add spinach to the veggies as a garnish.
9. Roast for another 8-10 minutes, or until the veggies are soft and the spinach is wilted.
10. Toss the veggies together and serve with the chicken.

GREEK LAMB CHOPS

INGREDIENTS

- **For the Marinade**
- Zest of 1 lemon
- 4 peppercorns
- ½ teaspoon dried oregano
- 1 tablespoon rosemary
- 8 lamb rib chops
- 1 ½ tablespoon mustard
- 1 tablespoon thyme
- 1 clove of garlic
- 1/3 of a cup olive oil
- **For the Potatoes**
- ½ teaspoon semolina
- Salt and pepper
- 1 teaspoon dried oregano
- Juice of 1 lemon
- 50ml olive oil
- 80ml water
- 1 large clove of garlic
- 4 potatoes

COOK TIME: 4 hours
SERVING: 4

INSTRUCTIONS

1. Combine all the marinade ingredients in a shallow glass baking dish and mix well.
2. Add the lamb chops and spread the marinade all over them.
3. Refrigerate for at least 3 hours after wrapping in plastic.
4. Preheat the oven to 200°C and bring the lamb chops back to room temperature.
5. Combine the ingredients for the potatoes in a mixing bowl.
6. Season the potatoes with salt and pepper after pouring the sauce over them.
7. Preheat the oven to 400°F and bake the potatoes for half an hour.
8. Return to the oven for another half an hour after adding a pinch of oregano.
9. Season the lamb chops with salt and pepper after removing them from the marinade.
10. In the same pan, roast the lamb chops for 25 minutes.
11. Allow 10 minutes for the Greek lamb chops to rest before serving with a squeeze of lemon and a sprinkling of dry oregano.

GREEK STUFFED SQUID

INGREDIENTS

- 1 teaspoon salt
- ½ teaspoon pepper
- 2 ¼ cups water
- ¾ cup rice
- 3 cloves garlic
- ¼ tablespoon parsley
- ½ cup olive oil
- 1 medium onion
- ½ tablespoon tomato paste
- ½ cup dry wine
- 2 ¼ pounds squid

COOK TIME: 95 mins
SERVING: 6

INSTRUCTIONS

1. Combine the tomato paste and wine in a medium-sized mixing bowl until smooth.
2. Preheat the oven to 350 degrees Fahrenheit.
3. Heat the olive oil and sauté the garlic, onion, and half of the minced tentacles in a large frying pan.
4. Combine the wine and tomato paste in a mixing bowl.
5. Cook, constantly stirring, until the mixture thickened slightly.
6. Bring half of the water to a boil in a separate pot.
7. Turn the heat down and stir in the rice.
8. Add salt & pepper to taste.
9. Fill the squid ducts with the rice filling using a little teaspoon.
10. Place in a baking sheet and secure it with one or more toothpicks.
11. Preheat the oven to 350°F and bake the squid for 1 hour and 10 minutes.
12. Before serving, gently remove toothpicks.

GREEK GRAVOS WITH PEPPERS

INGREDIENTS

- 1 teaspoon oregano
- 1 cup olive oil
- ½ cup parsley
- Salt and pepper
- 2 medium red onions
- 2 cloves, garlic
- 2 large ripe tomatoes
- 750 grams anchovies

COOK TIME: 1 hour
SERVING: 5

INSTRUCTIONS

1. Season anchovies with salt and black pepper.
2. Chop the onion, garlic, and parsley, then season with salt and oregano.
3. Cut the tomato in half and finely chop it before seasoning with salt.
4. In a baking pan, start with a layer of tomatoes.
5. Sprinkle part of the garlic, onion, and parsley combination over the top.
6. Arrange anchovies in a layer with the skin facing down.
7. Place the additional garlic, onions, parsley, and oregano in a large mixing bowl.
8. Add a final layer of tomatoes, salt, and oregano to finish.
9. Finally, drizzle the olive oil over the anchovies.
10. Bake in a preheated oven at 180° C for 45 minutes or until veggies are done without mixing or adding any water.
11. Serve over rice.

CUTTLEFISH WITH SPINACH

INGREDIENTS

- 1 tablespoon tomato paste
- 1 glass of water
- 10 sprigs of fennel
- 10 sprigs of dill
- 600g of spinach
- 4 spring onions
- 100 ml olive oil
- 500g cuttlefish

COOK TIME: 40 mins
SERVING: 6

INSTRUCTIONS

1. Drain and pat the cuttlefish dry with a dishtowel.
2. Heat half the olive oil in a deep saucepan, and sizzle the cuttlefish for 2-3 minutes.
3. Allow the chopped onion to sizzle before adding it to the pan.
4. Then add the tomato paste and continue to cook for a few minutes more.
5. Use wine to deglaze the pan.
6. Allow the spinach to wilt in the remaining olive oil, along with the fennel, chopped spinach, and dill.
7. Season with salt and pepper, and continue to stir gently for a few minutes more, or until most of the juices are disappeared.
8. Cover and simmer for half an hour on low to moderate heat till everything is properly combined.
9. Serve with fresh salad.

GREEK BEEF STEW

INGREDIENTS

- Salt and pepper
- A bit of water
- 4 allspice berries
- A pinch of nutmeg
- 1 tablespoon tomato paste
- 1 bay leaf
- 2 ripe tomatoes
- 14 oz. tomatoes
- 3 tablespoons red wine vinegar
- 1/3 of a cup cognac
- ¼ of a cup olive oil
- ¾ of a cup red wine
- 1.5 kg pearl onions
- 1 kg beef

COOK TIME: 2 hours
SERVING: 5

INSTRUCTIONS

1. Heat the oil in a saucepan, then add the meat and cook until browned on both sides.
2. Remove using a slotted spoon when done, transfer to a dish, cover, and set aside.
3. Peel and cut the onions crosswise, then add to the same oil used to brown the pork and sauté over medium heat.
4. Pour the wine, cognac, and red wine vinegar into the pan, cover, and cook for 3 minutes.
5. Pour the meat into the pot with its juices, add the tomato paste, and cook.
6. Stir the nutmeg, berries, allspice, bay leaf, diced tomatoes, and just enough water to cover the meat.
7. Bring the water to a boil.
8. Check to see whether the beef stifado needs more water while it is cooking.
9. Season with salt and pepper to taste after the cooking time.
10. Serve beef stifado with boiling new potatoes or pasta and shredded parmesan.

GREEK OCTUPUS WITH EGGPLANTS

INGREDIENTS

- **For the Octopus**
- 1 tablespoon peppercorns
- 50 g olive oil
- 3 onions
- 3 tablespoons vinegar
- 1 ½ kilo octopus
- **For the Salad**
- Salt
- Pepper
- ¼ bunch parsley
- 1 clove of garlic
- 2 tomatoes
- ¼ bunch mint
- 80 g olive oil
- 200 g manouri cheese
- 2 eggplants

COOK TIME: 40 mins
SERVING: 4

INSTRUCTIONS

1. Place the octopus on top of the onions.
2. Cover the surface of the saucepan with plastic wrap and add the peppercorns and vinegar.
3. Bring the saucepan to a boil over medium heat for 20-25 minutes.
4. Remove the saucepan from the heat and the plastic wrap with caution.
5. Remove the beak and slice the mantle of octopus.
6. Grease the mantle and tentacles with olive oil.
7. Grill until cooked through. Remove and set aside.
8. Grill the eggplant for 2 - 3 minutes on the grill.
9. Cut manouri cheese into slices and grill for 1 minute on each side.
10. Transfer the eggplant slices and manouri to a bowl after removing them from the heat.
11. Add the garlic, parsley, mint, and tomatoes to the bowl after finely chopping them.
12. Mix in the pepper, salt, and olive oil using a spoon.
13. Serve the octopus with the salad and lemon wedges on top.

GREEK ZUCCHINI FRITTERS

INGREDIENTS

- **For Fritters**
- Salt and pepper
- 4 tablespoons olive oil
- 4 large eggs
- 1 cup flour
- ½ teaspoon nutmeg
- 1 ½ cups crumbled feta
- 6 tablespoons dill
- 1 bunch scallions
- 3 cups zucchini
- **For Tzatziki**
- 1 tablespoon olive oil
- Salt and pepper
- ½ cup cucumber
- 1 teaspoon red wine vinegar
- 1 clove of garlic
- 2 cups Greek yogurt

COOK TIME: 40 mins
SERVING: 6

INSTRUCTIONS

1. Combine cucumber, garlic, yogurt, and vinegar or lime slices in a small bowl.
2. Add the olive oil and mix well.
3. Season to taste with salt and pepper.
4. Place a layer of paper towels on the counter and spread out the grated zucchini.
5. Salt zucchini and set aside for at least thirty minutes.
6. In a large mixing bowl, combine the drained zucchini, nutmeg, scallions, dill, and feta.
7. To blend, stir everything together.
8. Add the eggs and mix well.
9. Add salt & pepper to taste.
10. Add the flour and stir until the mixture combines together.
11. Make 3–4-inch patties out of the dough.
12. In a large pan, heat the olive oil over moderate flame.
13. Cook patties in a skillet until lightly brown on both sides and heated through but still moist.
14. Serve immediately with tzatziki on the side.

GREEK COD WITH GARLIC SAUCE

INGREDIENTS

- 5 teaspoons garlic
- ¼ cup Italian parsley leaves
- 1 ½ lb. cod fillet pieces
- **Crispy Coating**
- ½ teaspoon sea salt
- ½ teaspoon pepper
- 1 teaspoon paprika
- 1 teaspoon ground cumin
- 1 teaspoon coriander
- ⅓ cup all-purpose flour
- **Lemon Sauce**
- 5 tablespoons olive oil
- 2 tablespoons melted butter
- 5 tablespoons lemon juice

COOK TIME: 15 mins
SERVING: 6

INSTRUCTIONS

1. Preheat oven to 425 degrees Fahrenheit.
2. Combine the ingredients for the lemon sauce in a wide shallow bowl.
3. Mix the coating components in a second shallow wide bowl.
4. Using a paper towel, pat the cod fillets dry.
5. Set the fillets aside after dipping them in the lemon mixture and the flour mixture.
6. Pour two teaspoons of olive oil into a large pan set over medium-high heat.
7. Place fillets on a heated skillet and sear on each side for about 2-3 minutes.
8. Remove the pan from the heat.
9. Drizzle leftover lemon sauce over fillets with minced garlic.
10. Cook the fish for about 10 to 15 minutes in an oven-safe pan with the fillets inside.
11. Top cooked cod fillets with minced parsley.

GREEK CHEESE PIES

INGREDIENTS

- 2 tablespoons fresh mint
- Olive oil
- 100g ricotta cheese
- 2 large organic eggs
- 100g Parmesan
- 100g Gouda cheese
- 200g feta cheese
- ¾ of a cup heavy cream
- 10 sheets of phyllo pastry

COOK TIME: 85 mins
SERVING: 6

INSTRUCTIONS

1. Break the feta cheese with a fork into a large mixing bowl, then add the beaten eggs, the grated cheese, and the heavy cream.
2. Chop some fresh mint and toss it in with the other ingredients.
3. Season with freshly ground pepper and stir with a spoon until fully combined.
4. Refrigerate the mixture for at least 20 minutes.
5. Butter the bottom and sides of the tray using a pastry brush.
6. Place one sheet of phyllo in the bottom of the pan and drizzle with olive oil or melted butter using a cooking brush.
7. Repeat the procedure with another 4-5 sheets of phyllo dough.
8. With a spoon, smooth in the feta cheese mixture.
9. Fold the flaps of the extra phyllo sheets over the mixture.
10. Drizzle the top with butter or oil, then sprinkle with sesame seeds and water.
11. Preheat the oven to 180°C and bake the tiropita for 50 minutes.
12. Allow cooling for a few minutes before serving. Enjoy!

GREEK RICE WITH FISH

INGREDIENTS

- 1-pound raw shrimp
- 1 cup frozen peas
- ¼ teaspoon black pepper
- 1 cup mussels
- 2 tablespoons white wine
- ½ teaspoon salt
- 2 cups arborio rice
- ¼ cup leaf parsley
- 1 red bell pepper
- 1 yellow bell pepper
- 2 cups vegetable stock
- ½ cup olive oil
- 3 cups water

COOK TIME: 2 *hours*
SERVING: 6

INSTRUCTIONS

1. Put the water and veggie stock to a low simmer in a medium pot.
2. Set aside, covered.
3. Heat the olive oil in a big saucepan over medium-low heat and add the bell peppers.
4. Cook for 5 minutes or until softened.
5. Cook, stirring regularly, for two or three minutes after adding the rice and half of the parsley.
6. Deglaze the pan with the wine.
7. Then, whisk in the water/stock combination until everything is well combined.
8. Add salt & pepper to taste.
9. Lower the heat and cook for twenty minutes, covered.
10. Stir in the peas, mussels, and shrimp.
11. Cook for another 5 minutes, or until the shrimp are just cooked through.
12. Season with salt and pepper, then toss in the remaining parsley and serve.

GREEK BEEF AND ORZO STEW

INGREDIENTS

- 500g orzo pasta
- 100g kefalotyri cheese
- 1 cinnamon stick
- ½ cup of olive oil
- 1 teaspoon sugar
- 1 glass of red wine
- 1 tin tomatoes
- 2 tablespoons tomato paste
- 2 medium red onions
- 2 carrots
- 1 kg veal shoulder beef (veal)

COOK TIME: 60 mins
SERVING: 8

INSTRUCTIONS

1. In a skillet, heat the olive oil, then add the chopped onions and carrots and cook for 5 minutes over medium-low heat.
2. Increase the heat to high and add the veal.
3. After adding the tomato paste and sautéing for a minute, put in the red wine, combine the cinnamon stick, sugar, canned tomatoes, and salt and pepper in a large mixing bowl.
4. Reduce the heat to low and cook for 45 minutes with the cover on.
5. Meanwhile, heat another pan, add 3 tablespoons olive oil and sauté the orzo pasta until golden.
6. When the beef is simmering, combine the orzo pasta, meat, and sauce on an oven tray and stir well.
7. Cover the tray with aluminum foil and bake for half an hour at 180°C in a preheated oven.
8. Top with grated kefalotyri or other firm yellow cheese before serving.

GREEK SPINACH PIE

INGREDIENTS

- 8 sheets phyllo dough
- ¼ cup olive oil
- ½ cup ricotta cheese
- 1 cup crumbled feta cheese
- ½ cup parsley
- 2 eggs
- 2 cloves garlic
- 2 pounds spinach
- 1 large onion
- 1 bunch green onions
- 3 tablespoons olive oil

COOK TIME: 90 mins
SERVING: 5

INSTRUCTIONS

1. Preheat oven to 375 degrees Fahrenheit.
2. Heat 3 tablespoons of olive oil in a large pan over medium heat.
3. Sauté green onions, onion, and garlic until softened and gently browned.
4. Continue to sauté after adding the spinach and parsley.
5. Combine the ricotta, eggs, and feta in a medium mixing bowl.
6. Add the spinach mixture and stir well.
7. Brush 1 sheet of phyllo dough with olive oil and place in preheated baking pan.
8. Brush another layer of phyllo dough with olive oil and continue the process with two more sheets of phyllo dough.
9. Fold the excess dough over the spinach and cheese filling in the pan.
10. Bake for 30 minutes to an hour, until nicely browned in a preheated oven.
11. Serve immediately after cutting into squares.

Chapter 2: Macedonian Recipes

Traditional country food often catches a tourist's eye that always looks for new experiences on the overseas journey. The Republic of North Macedonia is a Balkan country with a unique culture and a long history. At the same time, it is a lifesaver for the hungry explorer of culinary delights. After being acquainted with Macedonian cuisine, the tourist's baggage will be refilled with amazing gastronomic experiences. The Macedonian food is healthy and nutritious. They use fresh fruits and vegetables to make their dishes. The use of olive oil makes it more appealing. Give a try to these easy recipes from Macedonian culture.

FRIED PASTRY WITH SYRUP

INGREDIENTS

- 5 large eggs
- 2 cups vegetable oil
- 3 ¼ cups all-purpose flour
- 1 tablespoon baking powder
- 6 tablespoons vegetable oil
- 2 cups water
- **Syrup**
- 2 ½ cups water
- 5 cups white sugar

COOK TIME: 3 hours
SERVING: 25

INSTRUCTIONS

1. In a large saucepan over medium temperature, bring 2 cups water and six tablespoons of oil to a boil.
2. Take the pan off the heat and stir in the flour and baking powder.
3. After that, beat the eggs with an electric mixer.
4. In a saucepan, combine the sugar and 2 cups water and cook over medium-high heat.
5. Stir until the sugar is completely dissolved.
6. While the syrup cools, heat the oil to 350 degrees F in a deep-fryer or big saucepan.
7. Pipe little quantities of dough into the heated oil using a tulumba syringe or an icing bag with a particular tip.
8. Fry tulumbas in batches until golden, about approximately five minutes.
9. Pour the cooled syrup over the tulumbas in a bowl.
10. Let rest for 10 minutes.
11. Serve with your favorite garnishes.

LAMB INTESTINES EASTER DELICACY

INGREDIENTS

- Salt
- Pepper
- 2 kilos of lamb bowels (Intestines)
- Oregano
- 2 caul fats
- The guts of two lambs

COOK TIME: 5 hours
SERVING: 20

INSTRUCTIONS

1. Drain the meat and season it with pepper, salt, and oregano before skewering it.
2. Add a bit of caul fat in between 2 or 3 pieces.
3. Wrap it with caul fat after it is cooked.
4. Wind the intestines around the skewers at the tip.
5. If the bowel comes to an end, tie it to the end of the next intestine.
6. The Kokoretsi and the Lamb on the spit are now ready to roast over charcoal.
7. When the chicken is fully cooked, remove it from the pan and serve with the sauce.

STUFFED LAMB'S STOMACH

INGREDIENTS

- 1 tablespoon tomato paste
- ¼ teaspoon saffron threads
- 1 rib celery
- 1 bottle dry white wine
- 1 medium onion
- 1 leek
- 3 tablespoons white wine vinegar
- 2 medium carrots
- 1 teaspoon Herbes de Provence
- 2 pounds beef honeycomb
- Coarse kosher salt
- 3 pig feet
- **Rope of Dough**
- 1 teaspoon vegetable oil
- ¾ cup flour

COOK TIME: 26 hours
SERVING: 6

INSTRUCTIONS

1. Put the tripe in a large pot with cold water and gently bring it to a boil.
2. Cook for fifteen minutes before draining.
3. Preheat the oven to 200 degrees Fahrenheit.
4. In a casserole, combine the veggies.
5. Combine the tomato paste, wine, herb bouquet, tripe, and saffron in a large mixing bowl.
6. Rinse and add the pig's feet or snouts to the saucepan.
7. To form a thick paste, add more water and oil to the flour.
8. To cook for 12 hours, place the pot on the center oven shelf.
9. Before discarding the veggies, push down on them with the back of a spoon to remove all the juices.
10. Let the fat in the cooking water rise to the surface.
11. Pour the broth over the pig's feet and tripe.
12. Serve with plenty of nice crusty bread on the side to soak up the meat juices while it's still hot.

Tip: If not serving right away, cover the bowl and store it in the refrigerator for up to three days.

SPINACH AND FETA BUREK

INGREDIENTS

- ½ cup of skim milk
- 10 Phyllo Dough sheets
- 2 tablespoons plain yogurt
- 3 tablespoons vegetable oil
- ¼ teaspoon black pepper
- 1 large egg
- ½ teaspoon salt
- **Filling**
- 2 tablespoons sesame seeds
- 1 cup feta cheese
- ¼ teaspoon salt
- ¼ teaspoon black pepper
- 1 onion
- 1 tablespoon olive oil
- 20 oz. baby spinach
- **Egg Wash**
- 2 egg yolks

COOK TIME: 60 mins
SERVING: 8

INSTRUCTIONS

1. Combine the salt, yogurt, egg, milk, olive oil, and pepper in a mixing dish.
2. Heat 1 tablespoon of olive oil in a large pan.
3. Cook for 3-5 minutes, or until the onion is aromatic.
4. Season with salt and pepper and add the spinach.
5. Strain it through a mesh strainer to remove all of the juices.
6. Place it in a mixing bowl with the feta cheese and gently swirl to incorporate.
7. Put two phyllo dough sheets on a baking sheet and brush with 3 tablespoons of the milk mixture.
8. Sprinkle the spinach-feta cheese mixture evenly over 1 sheet of phyllo dough.
9. Place 2 sheets of phyllo dough on top of each other and brush with 3 tablespoons of the milk mixture.
10. Brush the final phyllo dough with 2 tablespoons of the milk mixture and place it on top.
11. Cover it with plastic wrap, put it in the fridge, and let it be there for at least two hours or overnight.

TAVCE GRAVCE

INGREDIENTS

- 1 fresh pepper (garnish)
- 1 small-size onion
- 5 bay leaves
- Chopped parsley (garnish)
- 3 cloves of garlic
- 3 bouillon cubes
- ½ tablespoon of black pepper
- 1 tablespoon of cumin
- 2 onions
- 2 cups of tomato sauce
- 3 dried chili peppers
- 3 tablespoons of red pepper
- 5 tablespoons of sunflower oil
- 4 cups of beans

COOK TIME: 3 hours
SERVING: 4

INSTRUCTIONS

1. Combine the beans, bay leaves, bouillon cubes, chili peppers, onions, and red pepper in a large pot.
2. Cook the beans over medium heat.
3. Remove the leaves and drain the beans.
4. Remove the skillet from the oven and coat it with sunflower oil.
5. Mix some red pepper with the sunflower oil until the oil and paprika are evenly distributed.
6. Preheat the oven to 190°C and add coarsely diced celery and crushed garlic cloves to the mix.
7. Toss the beans with 1 tablespoon of tomato sauce and 1 teaspoon of salt.
8. Pour off part of the water and add the beans.
9. Allow one hour in the oven.
10. Place some fresh peppers on top of the dish.
11. For 5 minutes, raise the temperature to 220 °C.
12. As a garnish, sprinkle peppers, onions, and parsley on top.

POTATO STEW

INGREDIENTS

- 300 ml veg stock
- 2 tablespoons cacao powder
- 3 bay leaves
- 2 400g tins tomatoes
- 1 can green lentils
- 1 stem of rosemary
- 3 celery stalks
- 500 g baby potatoes
- ¼ cup tamari
- 4 carrots
- 1 red onion
- 350 g mushrooms
- 3 large garlic cloves

COOK TIME: 40 mins
SERVING: 5

INSTRUCTIONS

1. Heat the olive oil in a big saucepan.
2. Combine the mushrooms, onion, garlic, and tamari in a large mixing bowl.
3. Cook for 5 minutes, stirring occasionally.
4. Combine the vegetable stock, tomatoes, bay leaves, rosemary, lentils, potatoes, celery, and carrots in a large mixing bowl.
5. Stir in the cacao powder until everything is fully combined.
6. Simmer for half an hour with the cover on the pot.
7. Serve with white rice or quinoa and fresh parsley on the side.

Tip: You can keep this in the fridge for a few days in an airtight container or freeze it for later.

Chapter 3: Recipes from Cyprus

A wide variety of native herbal components are used in Cyprus culinary creations. Vegetables, fruits, herbs, and other plants thrive in Cyprus' moderate temperate, subtropical environment. Meat items consist of pig and lamb that are considered typical products of Cyprus cattle farming. Milk and milk derivatives are frequently used in the food of Cyprus chefs. Extensive pastures and meadows enable large dairy products to be used in the cuisine. Make these delicious recipes from Cyprus food culture.

SAGANAKI FRIED HALLOUMI CHEESE

INGREDIENTS

- 1 teaspoon dried oregano
- Black pepper
- 2 tablespoons clear honey
- 1 teaspoon black sesame seeds
- 1 small egg
- 3 tablespoons fine semolina
- 8oz. block halloumi
- 3 tablespoons olive oil

COOK TIME: 40 mins
SERVING: 4

INSTRUCTIONS

1. In a nonstick frying pan, heat the olive oil.
2. Cut halloumi horizontally across the center.
3. Roll the halloumi slices in the semolina after dipping them in the beaten egg.
4. Fry for a few minutes on each side over moderate flame until nicely browned.
5. Warm the honey in a separate small pan.
6. Serve the halloumi slices into squares with hot honey drizzled on top and oregano, sesame seeds, and black pepper on top.

ZUCCHINI SCRAMBLED EGGS WITH HALLOUMI

INGREDIENTS

- 4 large eggs
- 4 ounces halloumi cheese
- 1 tablespoon fresh mint
- 1 tablespoon fresh dill
- 1 large zucchini
- Salt and black pepper
- 1 tablespoon olive oil

COOK TIME: 25 mins
SERVING: 2

INSTRUCTIONS

1. In a small oven-safe skillet, heat the olive oil over medium heat.
2. Cook until zucchini is tender, approximately 5 minutes, with a touch of salt.
3. Cook for another minute after adding the chopped mint and dill.
4. Whisk together eggs, salt, and pepper in a small bowl.
5. Stir slightly before pouring into the heated skillet with the zucchini.
6. As the edges of the frittata begin to firm, place Halloumi slices on top.
7. Put the skillet underneath the broiler for about 5 minutes, or until the top of the frittata is entirely set and the cheese is slightly browned.
8. Serve hot or cold, depending on your preference.

KOUPES ROLLS FROM CYPRUS

INGREDIENTS

- **For the Coating**
- 2 eggs
- Olive oil for frying
- ½ teaspoon black pepper
- 3 coffee mugs, hot water
- 1 teaspoon salt
- 500 g Bulgar wheat
- **For the Filling**
- Olive oil for frying
- 3 large fresh lemons
- 2 teaspoons dried mint
- Parsley leaf
- 1 tsp dried oregano
- 1 teaspoon garlic puree
- 1 teaspoon black pepper
- ¼ teaspoon cinnamon powder
- 2 medium onions
- 2 teaspoons sea salt
- 500 g pork mince

COOK TIME: 60 mins
SERVING: 4

INSTRUCTIONS

1. Fill a large mixing bowl halfway with boiling water and add the pepper, salt, and bulgar wheat.
2. Set the timer for 1 hour.
3. Remove any surplus water.
4. After the eggs are cooled, add them to the batter and blend everything with a stick blender.
5. Heat a little olive oil in a skillet and cook the pork mince over moderate flame.
6. Combine the garlic, oregano, pepper, salt, and mint in a mixing bowl.
7. Cook until the onions are thoroughly softened, then add the diced onions.
8. Add a large handful of fresh parsley, chopped.
9. Soak your hands and spoon out a little amount of bulgar wheat mixture, roughly the size of a golf ball and a half.
10. Pour in about 2 tablespoons of the filling.
11. Put a few balls into the oil in a small frying pan over high heat.
12. Allow for browning.
13. Using a slotted spatula, remove and set it on kitchen paper to drain.
14. Garnish with a slice of lemon after they are all done.

CYPRUS ARMY PORK CHOPS

INGREDIENTS

- **Meat**
- 1 pork chop
- **Spices (to your taste)**
- 1 Bay leaf
- ½ teaspoon Marjorie herbs
- ½ teaspoon Cinnamon powder
- Pepper
- Cumin powder
- ½ teaspoon Coriander crushed
- Salt
- 1 teaspoon Oregano
- **Marinating Juices**
- Olive oil
- Dry Red wine

COOK TIME: 2 hours
SERVING: 4

INSTRUCTIONS

1. Pour the wine and olive oil over the chops until it reaches the smallest rib-brim.
2. Add spices to the oil.
3. Grab the tray with the liquids inside and carefully swirl the spices around horizontally.
4. Add the Bay leaves on top of the meat in the same pan with spices.
5. Cover the tray in tin foil when you are done with each chop.
6. Remove the cling wrap from the contents and place them in the oven.
7. Cook for about 1 hour at 375F temperature.
8. Serve with your favorite sauce.

CYPRIOT STYLE FRIES

INGREDIENTS

- 1 tablespoon lemon juice
- 1 teaspoon oregano
- Oil as needed
- Salt
- 2 lb. (1 kg) potatoes

COOK TIME: 45 mins
SERVING: 4

INSTRUCTIONS

1. Clean the potatoes, peel them, coarsely chop them, wash them again, and drain them.
2. Season with a pinch of salt and a squeeze of lemon juice.
3. Then fry until they are approximately 80% done, remove them from the oil to cool, and put them in the fridge for about 2 hours.
4. Fry till golden brown, then remove from the oil and season with oregano.

TRADITIONAL TOASTED CYPRUS SANDWICH

INGREDIENTS

- 3 triares sesame buns
- Pinch of salt
- 2 cucumbers
- 100g piccalilli
- 200g lountza
- 2 large tomatoes
- 2 halloumi

COOK TIME: 25 mins
SERVING: 3

INSTRUCTIONS

1. Lightly sauté the Lountza and Halloumi in a skillet, aiming for a light golden color.
2. Set aside for now.
3. To create a light golden hue, slice the bananas without separating them and cook them in the same pan.
4. To assemble the buns, set them on your work surface and smear piccalilli on the bottom side of each one.
5. Then layer the Lountza slices on top of them, one on top of the other.
6. Place the Halloumi slices on top, closely next to each other.
7. Toss in the tomato and cucumber slices, one on top of the other.
8. Season lightly with salt, then flip the bun over and carefully press the sandwich together.
9. Cut in half and serve with additional piccalilli on the side.

Chapter 4: Cretan Recipes

Crete is a complicated and powerful island off the coast of mainland Greece, with a rugged, hilly landscape and a strong cultural tradition. Cretan cuisine is known for its distinct ingredients and flavors in Greece and abroad. The variety of local products characterizes the recipes based on basic techniques. It includes mountain herbs and vegetables, bulbs, distinctive cheeses, raw seafood, the famed Cretan oil, and raki, a refreshing grape liquor. Have a look at these Cretan recipes.

CRETAN DAKOS

INGREDIENTS

- Black pepper, to taste
- Pinch Greek oregano
- 3 tablespoons feta cheese
- 3 teaspoons olive oil
- 1 large tomato
- ½-pound barley rusk

COOK TIME: 15 mins
SERVING: 4

INSTRUCTIONS

1. To moisten the hard rusks, spray them with water.
2. Shred the tomato into a colander over a bowl using a vegetable grater, allowing most of the liquid to drain.
3. Spread the strained, shredded tomato and sprinkle with cheese on the rusk.
4. Splash with olive oil and season with pepper and a generous quantity of oregano.

Tip: Add another couple of thinly sliced green pepper and onion if desired.

BRAISED CRETAN LAMB

INGREDIENTS

- Juice of 6 lemons
- 6 egg yolks
- 1 large bouquet dill
- 1 bouquet mint
- 1 pack large spinach
- 1 bunch Swiss chard
- 1 bunch dandelion greens
- 1 bunch kale leaves
- 1 tablespoon Greek oregano
- Black pepper
- 2 cups olive oil
- 1 tablespoon sea salt
- 5 medium onions
- 5 lbs. lamb shoulder

COOK TIME: 60 mins
SERVING: 5

INSTRUCTIONS

1. Combine oregano, salt, lamb, olive oil, chopped onions, and pepper in a big pan.
2. Place over moderate flame until the meat blanch but does not brown.
3. Pour in just enough hot water to cover the ingredients.
4. Bring the water to a boil.
5. Chop all of the leaves.
6. Heat for 5 minutes with the lid on.
7. Add the dill and mint to the pan and stir softly when the raw leaves are done.
8. Meanwhile, whisk together the yolks and lemon juice in a mixing dish.
9. To temper the mixture, slowly pour up to three tablespoons of the cooking water into a small bowl with the eggs, then pour into the hot pan.
10. To integrate and blend the sauce, swirl the pan in a clockwise direction for about 2 minutes.
11. Remove from the fire and set aside for 10 minutes, uncovered. Serve with rice.

CRETAN CUCUMBER & TOMATO SALAD

INGREDIENTS

- 1 teaspoon oregano
- Sea salt and black pepper
- ⅓ cup olive oil
- ¼ cup red wine vinegar
- 100g barley rusks
- 100g Anthotyro cheese
- 100g green capsicum
- 100g small red onion
- 300g Lebanese cucumbers
- 500g truss tomatoes

COOK TIME: 10 mins
SERVING: 6

INSTRUCTIONS

1. Cut the barley rusks into small pieces and scatter the veggies with anthotyro cheese crumbles.
2. Season with salt and pepper after adding the red wine vinegar, olive oil, and oregano.
3. Toss until well blended, then taste and adjust spices as needed.
4. Place everything in a salad dish and serve.

Tip: Greek superstores sell barley rusks, which you can replace with bagel chips or create yourself with wholemeal sourdough.

CRETAN VILLAGE SALAD

INGREDIENTS

- 200g Greek feta
- ½ teaspoon Greek oregano
- 20 black olives
- 125ml olive oil
- 1 Spanish onion
- 1 cup purslane
- 2 Lebanese cucumbers
- 2 vine-ripened tomatoes

COOK TIME: 15 mins
SERVING: 4

INSTRUCTIONS

1. Toss together the olives, purslane, onion, barley rusk, cucumber, tomato, and olive oil in a mixing bowl, seasoning to taste.
2. Arrange on a dish, top with feta, drizzle with more oil, and sprinkle with Greek oregano before serving.

CRETAN EGGS WITH WILD WEEDS

INGREDIENTS

- 4 eggs
- Pide bread to serve
- 1 teaspoon black pepper
- 1 teaspoon hot paprika
- 80ml olive oil
- 1 teaspoon salt
- 3 spring onions
- 1 onion
- 1 cup of mixed vegetables

COOK TIME: 25 mins
SERVING: 4

INSTRUCTIONS

1. In a nonstick deep fryer, heat the olive oil over a moderate flame, then add the onion and cook for 5 minutes.
2. Cook for another 60 seconds with the spring onions before adding the wild greens.
3. Allow for around 5 minutes of light frying to allow any extra water to evaporate.
4. Toss in the spices and mix well.
5. Break an egg into each of the four wells in the mixture.
6. Cook until the eggs are set, but the centers are still runny about 5 minutes.
7. Serve alongside pide.

CRETAN CHEESE MEZE WITH SUN DRIED TOMATOES

INGREDIENTS

- 1 teaspoon red pepper flakes
- 6 slices tomatoes
- 1 teaspoon thyme
- 1 teaspoon chili pepper
- 1 handful parsley
- 1 teaspoon dried mint
- ½ cup walnuts
- 2 tablespoons olive oil
- 250 g crumbled feta cheese

COOK TIME: 40 mins
SERVING: 4

INSTRUCTIONS

1. Mix sun-dried tomatoes and boiling water in a mixing bowl, put aside for fifteen minutes, then drain.
2. Dice the softened sun-dried tomatoes.
3. In a small saucepan, heat the olive oil, add the chili, and cook for 1-2 seconds before removing from the heat.
4. With a fork, mince the feta cheese.
5. In a mixing bowl, combine sun-dried tomatoes, pepper flakes, thyme, dried mint, parsley, walnuts, cheese, olive oil, and chili sauce. Serve right away.

Chapter 5: Aegean Islands Recipes

With their tempting indigenous fragrances and delectable flavors, your adventures throughout the Aegean Sea will melt your heart. Welcome to the realm of flavor on the Aegean Sea: As you follow gastronomic map of the area, you will find red and rich white sauces, tenderly cooked pulses, tasty home-grown veggies from historically fertile soil, bread, and pies with the rigorous flavor of local barley and wheat variations, and fresh goat cheeses. The pies are mostly wrapped in these kinds of cheese with thin dough. Make these recipes to taste the Aegean Island dishes.

ISLAND OMELET

INGREDIENTS

- 8 kalamata olives
- Dash of black pepper
- 1-ounce feta cheese
- 6 eggs
- 1 can artichoke hearts
- 1 medium tomato
- ¼ cup onion
- 9-ounce spinach

COOK TIME: 25 mins
SERVING: 3

INSTRUCTIONS

1. Preheat the pan over medium heat, coated with cooking spray.
2. Cook and stir onions for 2 minutes, or until crisp-tender.
3. Heat the artichoke hearts.
4. Toss in the tomatoes, spinach, and feta cheese for a few seconds.
5. Remove the pan from the heat and set it aside.
6. Wipeout and re-spray the skillet when it cooled.
7. In a medium mixing bowl, whisk together the eggs and pepper; add the olives.
8. Preheat the skillet to medium-high heat.
9. Cook the egg mixture for around 5-7 minutes.
10. When the egg mixture is set, spread half of the vegetable mixture over the omelet with a spatula, loosen the omelet, and fold it in half.
11. Remove the omelet from the pan and place it on a serving platter.

ISLAND SALAD WITH CHICKENA & AVOCADO

INGREDIENTS

- 2 tablespoons black kalamata olives
- Pitta bread, to serve
- Flatleaf parsley
- 5 tablespoons olive oil
- ½ teaspoon oregano
- ½ teaspoon mint
- 3 tablespoons lemon juice
- 200g packet feta cheese
- 3 spring onions
- 2 ripe avocados
- 2 hearts romaine lettuces
- 4 tomatoes
- 1.8kg roasted chicken

COOK TIME: 50 mins
SERVING: 6

INSTRUCTIONS

1. Toss the feta cheese with the dry oregano and mint, crumbling it with your fingers.
2. Remove the parsley leaves and set them aside.
3. Whisk 3 tablespoons lemon juice, sea salt, olive oil, and pepper together.
4. Toss the tomatoes, lettuce, chicken, and spring onion in a large mixing bowl, then fold the dressing in three parts with the avocados.
5. Season with salt and pepper, then spread the feta, olives, and parsley over the top and drizzle with the remaining dressing.
6. Serve with pita bread if desired and more lemon juice squeezed on top.

ISLANDS QUINOA SALAD

INGREDIENTS

- ½ teaspoon salt
- 1 cup Island dressing
- 2 tablespoons olive oil
- 1 tablespoon lemon juice
- ½ cup mint leaves
- 1 cup avocado
- ¼ cup cucumber
- ¼ cup carrots
- 1 cup cherry tomatoes
- 1 cup Arugula leaves
- 1 cup green peas
- 1 cup canned corn
- 1¼ cup Quinoa
- 1 chili pepper

COOK TIME: 30 mins
SERVING: 4

INSTRUCTIONS

1. Cook the quinoa according to the package directions in a saucepan for 15 minutes.
2. Allow sitting for 5 minutes before draining.
3. Combine the island dressing, olive oil, lemon, and salt in a small mixing bowl.
4. Fill 4 jars evenly with the mixture.
5. Then add the quinoa and green peas.
6. Corn, cherry tomatoes, cucumber, chili slices, mint leaves, and avocado are good additions.
7. Serve with arugula leaves on top.
8. Before serving, give the jars a good shake. Enjoy!

ISLANDS GRILLED BREAD AND TOMATOES

INGREDIENTS

- Black pepper
- ½ cup herb leaves
- 24 small Kalamata olives
- ¼ cup scallions
- 1 cucumber
- ¼-pound feta cheese
- 6 slices ciabatta
- 2 pounds ripe tomatoes
- 1 ½ teaspoons garlic
- Kosher salt
- 1 tablespoon sherry vinegar
- 3 tablespoons olive oil

COOK TIME: 2 hours
SERVING: 8

INSTRUCTIONS

1. Mix 3 tablespoons olive oil, garlic, sherry vinegar, and a sprinkle of salt in a small bowl.
2. Preheat a gas grill or a broiler to medium-high.
3. Cook until the slices are light golden brown, right on the grill grate.
4. In a large mixing bowl, combine the fresh pepper, salt, scallions, olives, feta, cucumbers, tomatoes, and half of the herbs.
5. Toss in the bread cubes lightly to incorporate.
6. Toss the salad gently but completely with the olive oil vinegar combination.
7. Season with salt and pepper to taste.
8. Enable rest for fifteen minutes to let the bread soak some of the tomato juices, tossing once.
9. Serve in a small serving dish with the leftover herbs on top.

ISLAND SHRIMP WITH PASTA

INGREDIENTS

- ¾ cup hot water
- 1 teaspoon salt
- Pasta of your choice
- 1 tablespoon olive oil
- 3-pound shrimp
- Pasta sauce as needed

COOK TIME: 30 mins
SERVING: 4

INSTRUCTIONS

1. Fill a big saucepan with boiling water to a third.
2. Cover with a lid after adding salt.
3. Bring the water to a boil.
4. Cook pasta for 10-12 minutes, or until desired softness is reached.
5. Drain, return to pot and toss to coat with olive oil.
6. Meanwhile, bring the sauce to a boil in a sauté pan.
7. Reduce the heat to low and cook for 7 minutes.
8. Rinse and clean shrimp, then add to sauce and cook for 1-2 minutes, or until they turn pink.
9. Cook until the feta and olives are warmed thoroughly.
10. Serve right immediately over spaghetti.

SHRIMP RECIPE WITH TOMATO AND FETA

INGREDIENTS

- ¾ teaspoon oregano
- 2 tablespoons fresh mint
- 1-½ pounds shrimp
- 6 ounces feta cheese
- ½ teaspoon red pepper flakes
- 1 tablespoon honey
- ¼ teaspoon pepper
- 1 teaspoon cumin
- 1 (28-oz) can of tomatoes
- 1 teaspoon salt
- ¾ cup shallots
- 4 garlic cloves
- 4 tablespoons olive oil

COOK TIME: 50 mins
SERVING: 4

INSTRUCTIONS

1. Preheat the oven to 400 degrees Fahrenheit.
2. In a large oven-safe skillet, heat the olive oil over medium-low heat.
3. Cook the shallots and garlic together.
4. Combine the tomatoes, juices, red pepper flakes, cumin, pepper, salt, and honey in a large mixing bowl.
5. Bring to the boil, then lower to medium-low and continue to simmer.
6. Remove the shrimp from the heat and distribute them equally over the tomato sauce.
7. Sprinkle the oregano over the feta and sprinkle the feta over the prawns.
8. Bake for 12–15 minutes, or until the shrimp are pinkish and cooked through.
9. Allow 5 minutes for the shrimp to settle before serving with mint.

Chapter 6: Recipes from Ionian Islands

The sun, the sea, and the energizing breezes have sculpted the Ionian Islands. Culinary traditions in the area extend back to prehistoric times and are an integral component of the culture. Oregano, basil, bay leaves, oregano, and olive oil are high-quality ingredients with earthy scents. The microclimate of each island has aided in the development of tasty produce, some of which are unique to the globe. In this last chapter, I have included some Ionian Island recipes for you to must try.

POLENTA

INGREDIENTS

- 200g instant polenta
- 100g smoked cheese
- 1 tablespoon tomato purée
- 4 rosemary sprigs
- 400g can chopped tomato
- 200ml chicken stock
- 1 garlic clove
- 6 pork sausages
- 1 onion
- 1 tablespoon olive oil

COOK TIME: 25 mins
SERVING: 4

INSTRUCTIONS

1. Sauté the onion and garlic in the oil in a frying pan casserole dish over intermediate heat for a few minutes.
2. Cook for another 8-9 minutes after adding the sausages; split them up into little bits as you go.
3. In a large mixing bowl, combine the purée, stock, diced tomatoes, and the majority of the rosemary.
4. Bring to a boil, then reduce to low heat and cook for another 8-10 minutes, or until the sauce is thickened.
5. Season with salt and pepper to taste.
6. Meanwhile, prepare the polenta according to the package directions.
7. Remove the pan from the heat and add the cheese, along with a pinch of salt and pepper.
8. Distribute the polenta among four dishes, then top with the ragout and the remaining rosemary.

SKORDOSTOUMBI

INGREDIENTS

- 1 teaspoon honey
- 5 tablespoons feta
- ⅔ cup fresh herbs
- 3 tablespoons sherry vinegar
- 5 large tomatoes
- Black pepper to taste
- 2/3 cup olive oil
- 10 garlic cloves
- Salt to taste
- 3 medium eggplants

COOK TIME: 1 hour
SERVING: 4

INSTRUCTIONS

1. Gently salt the eggplant pieces in a mixing bowl.
2. Heat 2 to 3 tablespoons olive oil over the moderate flame in a big, heavy skillet.
3. Using paper towels, absorb any excess liquid.
4. Preheat oven to 375 degrees Fahrenheit.
5. Add the garlic to the same deep fryer and sauté for a few moments, just to soften it.
6. Add the tomato, simmer for a few minutes over medium heat, season with salt and black pepper, and then add the honey and vinegar.
7. Cook, occasionally stirring, until the sauce is thickened, about 20 to 25 minutes.
8. Drizzle a little olive oil over a few teaspoons of the sauce in the bottom of a large baking dish.
9. Sprinkle the herbs and a little cheese if preferred.
10. Apply a small layer of sauce to the eggplant and keep layering until all of the sauce has been used up.
11. Pour a little vinegar over the top and press it down with a spatula.
12. Bake for 45 minutes, then remove from the oven, top with chopped parsley, and serve with creamy polenta, feta, or both.

CORFU DELICIOUS BIANCO

INGREDIENTS

- Black pepper
- 100 grams olive oil
- 100 grams lemon juice
- 3 potatoes
- 4 cloves garlic
- 4 medium-sized fish

COOK TIME: 60 mins
SERVING: 4

INSTRUCTIONS

1. Combine the oil, 2 cups of water, garlic, and add a teaspoon of sweet pepper in a pan.
2. If we do not fill in more, the fish and potatoes will almost be completely covered by the water.
3. If the fish is not salted, season with salt.
4. Then boil everything over a normal heat until there is no more water.
5. Check the taste; season with salt, then squeeze in the lemon juice.
6. Allow barely half a minute before removing it from the fire.
7. It will be ready to serve in 2 minutes if you cover it.

NOSTIMO FAGITO

INGREDIENTS

- Salt and pepper
- 1 small rusk
- 1 teaspoon dried wild oregano
- Aleppo chili flakes as needed
- 40g parmesan cheese
- 400g large tomatoes
- Grated zest of 1 lemon
- 120g mozzarella
- 500ml vegetable stock
- Large sprig oregano
- 250g orzo
- 1 tablespoon tomato puree
- 1 red onion
- 3 large cloves of garlic
- 2 tablespoons olive oil
- 300g garden eggs

COOK TIME: 60 mins
SERVING: 4

INSTRUCTIONS

1. Remove the tips of the garden eggs and cut them in half lengthwise.
2. Boil for 8-10 minutes in water, then drain and deseed with a spoon.
3. Meanwhile, heat the olive oil in a separate pan and sauté the onions until tender and golden.
4. Cook for a few more minutes after adding the chili flakes, garlic, and garden eggs.
5. Stir in the orzo and tomato puree and mix to coat.
6. Combine the fresh oregano, wine, stock, and zest in a large mixing bowl.
7. Cut the mozzarella into bits and top with grated parmesan cheese.
8. Add salt & pepper to taste. Slice the tomatoes 1cm thick and arrange them on top to cover the rice.
9. Bake for half an hour, stirring gently midway through it without breaking the tomatoes, sprinkled with dry oregano and crushed rusk.
10. Serve with olives and a simple green salad.

FRIED ANCHOVIES

INGREDIENTS

- 1 lemon
- 1 French baguette
- 1 cup white flour
- 2 teaspoons salt
- 2 cups olive oil
- 1-pound anchovies

COOK TIME: 15 mins
SERVING: 4

INSTRUCTIONS

1. Pour the olive oil in a large frying pan.
2. Heat the oil over moderate flame.
3. Place the flour on a large dinner plate and add about 2 tablespoons of salt while the oil is heated.
4. Roll the anchovies in the flour one by one covering them on all sides.
5. Cook the fish in batches until golden brown, flipping once.
6. Remove the anchovies from the pan with a slotted spoon and set them on top of paper towels to absorb any leftover oil.
7. Season to taste, then season with a little salt if necessary.
8. Serve with baguette pieces and lemon wedges.

MACARONI CHEESE

INGREDIENTS

- 2 cups milk
- 2 cups Cheddar cheese
- ½ teaspoon salt
- Black pepper to taste
- ¼ cup butter
- ¼ cup all-purpose flour
- 1 (8 ounces) box macaroni

COOK TIME: 30 mins
SERVING: 4

INSTRUCTIONS

1. Bring a big saucepan of lightly salted water to a boil.
2. Cook 8 minutes in boiling water, turning periodically until elbow macaroni is cooked through but hard to bite.
3. Melt the butter in a saucepan over medium heat; whisk in the flour, salt, and pepper until homogeneous, about 5 minutes.
4. Slowly add milk into the butter-flour mixture, constantly stirring, until smooth and bubbly for about 5 minutes.
5. Stir in the Cheddar cheese until completely melted for about two to four minutes.
6. Toss the macaroni with the cheese sauce until it is well covered. Serve immediately.

Conclusion

Food is a physical representation of affection and hospitality. Cooking, the procedure and rituals that go along with it are something that Greeks adore. In this regard, Greek culinary culture may be intense. As you can see, eating Greek meals not only gives you delicious food that is also highly nutritious, but it also allows you to indulge in delicacies that have been around for hundreds of years. The unusual spices will leave an indelible stamp on everything you try, and each dish's local food and cleanliness will overpower your senses. Greek cuisine will leave an indelible impression on you whatever meals you try.

GREEK

COOKBOOK

60 Recipes for Traditional Food from
Greece

Adele Tyler

Introduction

Greek food has a long and rich history and is famous for various meals, including tender meat dishes, spicy salads, fresh seafood, and sweet desserts. Greece's coastline and islands, being Europe's southern country, have a Mediterranean climate suitable for farming and vineyards. Furthermore, for the past ten thousand years, its location on the Aegean has allowed direct access to fresh fish. High-quality ingredients, herbs, and well-held family traditions characterize traditional Greek cuisine.

While Greek food has affected and been impacted by other civilizations, Greece is at the top of the list of countries with a "blended" cuisine dating back to 300 B.C. Hummus, Tzatziki, and dolmades, which can be discovered in restaurants from Armenia to Egypt, have found a home in Greek food preparation and adjusted to tastes and traditions over hundreds of years.

Classic aspects of Greek cuisine were also adopted and modified across boundaries throughout that period, in Europe, Northern Africa, the Mideast, and the far east. Greek food is one of the world's largest, healthiest, and most well-rounded cuisines. Greece's gastronomic peculiarities are unique to each city, town, community, and island. Regional meals are perhaps the greatest way to get a flavor of the local produce.

Greeks enjoy meat, but they also recognize the need for a well-balanced diet. A huge, tangy salad is a must-have for any typical Greek supper. The "xoriatiki Salata," or village salad, is the most traditional Greek salad. Tomatoes, cucumber, parmesan cheese, shallots, garlic, and olive oil are common ingredients in this salad. Although the village salad is the most popular dish, Greece offers a variety of vegetarian-friendly choices.

Fish and seafood are prominent and frequently used elements of Greek cuisine, as 20 percent of Greece is comprised of islands, and no section of the Greek mainland is more than eighty miles from the sea. Lamb and goats are the typical meats of festivals and celebrations, although plenty of chicken, beef, and pig is also used.

Much of Greece's mountainous landscape is covered in vineyards, and the country is recognized for its exquisite wines and most famously ouzo, a slightly sweet liqueur that is the official drink.

Greek has largely delicious, uncomplicated food that effectively incorporates all of the land and marine foods that flourish under the scorching heat and gentle air. Perhaps this is why Greek cuisine suits us so well and is customized to our needs.

Even though the Greek people are bonded by a common language, a common history, and traditional food, each area takes pleasure in its unique folklore: traditional attire, regional dialects, and, of course, regional cuisine. Each region has its distinct cuisine based on regional culinary customs. Only a small percentage of Greeks work in agriculture, like any other developed nation. Even those who previously had a few grapes, olive trees, greeneries, and maybe a sheep or two in the back gardens have generally left the countryside — some for the city, and others, particularly on the numerous islands.

Many people, particularly those who live on the islands and villages, have a strong emotional attachment to the land and its cuisine. They raise their vegetables and fruit, gather honey, herd goats and sheep, extract the tsipouro they drink, search for wild herbs, and prepare with olives oil made from their olives.

It is astonishing how little we know about this country and its food. Let's take a tour of Greek food through this Greek Cookbook.

Chapter 1: Classic and Famous Greek Dishes

Greece is a country of small farmers that create an extraordinary variety of mostly organic cheese, cereals, legumes, fats, berries, nuts, veggies, and a variety of wild plants and herbs. These are the items that make up the traditional Greek diet, and they give diversity and health to it. The climate in Greece is ideal for cultivating olive and citrus trees, which provide two of the most significant ingredients in Greek cuisine. Spices, cloves, and other herbs like rosemary, mint, basil, and thyme, as well as vegetables like eggplant and zucchini, and beans of all kinds, are commonly utilized. Here are some famous recipes from Greek cuisine.

SKORDALIA

INGREDIENTS

- ½ cup water
- 1 tablespoon salt
- 2 tablespoons red wine vinegar
- ½ cup olive oil
- 7 cloves of garlic
- 6 medium potatoes

COOK TIME: 40 *mins*
SERVING: 8

INSTRUCTIONS

1. Bring a saucepan of cold water to a boil with the potatoes.
2. Reduce the heat to a low-medium heat and cook for half an hour.
3. Combine red wine vinegar, garlic, hot water, and salt in a food processor.
4. Blend until the garlic is completely dissolved.
5. Cut the potatoes into small pieces and mix them in a food processor.
6. Pour in the extra virgin olive oil.
7. Blend until the oil is all integrated and the liquid is silky smooth.
8. Serve the skordalia as a delightful dip or side dish with some toasted bread or pita bread. Enjoy!

Tip: To make skordalia, boil the potatoes until they are very soft.

GREEK HONEY COOKIES

INGREDIENTS

- **For the Melomakarona**
- 50g honey
- zest of 2 oranges
- 125g olive oil
- 125g vegetable oil
- ½ tablespoon baking soda
- 90g water
- 150g fine semolina
- 1/3 teaspoon clove
- 1 teaspoon vanilla extract
- 1 flat tablespoon cinnamon
- 1/3 teaspoon nutmeg
- 3 tablespoons cognac
- 100g sugar
- ½ tablespoon baking powder
- 100g orange juice
- 500g flour
- **For the Syrup**
- 1 orange
- 200g honey
- 2 cinnamon sticks
- 3 whole cloves
- 600g sugar
- 300g water

COOK TIME: 50 mins
SERVING: 50 pieces

INSTRUCTIONS

1. Bring all of the components for the syrup, except the honey, to a boil in a saucepan.
2. Set aside after adding the honey.
3. Mix the flour, semolina, and baking powder in a mixing dish.
4. Mix the sugar, cognac, orange juice, and spices (clove, cinnamon, nutmeg, vanilla) in a separate large mixing bowl.
5. Whisk in the baking soda.
6. Whisk together the oil, the water, the orange zest, and the honey in a mixing bowl.
7. In the same bowl, combine the mixed semolina, flour, and baking powder with honey mixture.
8. Make the dough by kneading it.
9. Preheat the oven to 180 degrees Celsius.
10. Form the dough into a ball and set it on the baking sheet.
11. Place the melomakarona baking pans and bake for about 20 minutes.
12. Dip the melomakarona in the cool syrup as soon as they come out of the oven.
13. Using a slotted spoon, remove the cookies.

Tip: Keep the melomakarona in an airtight jar at room temperature. They will last you through all of your Christmas holidays!

GREEK BAKED ORZO

INGREDIENTS

- 2 ½ cups vegetable broth
- 2 tablespoons butter
- 1 14-ounce can tomato
- 2 cups chickpeas
- 3 tablespoons tomato paste
- 1 cup uncooked orzo
- Pinch of red pepper flakes
- 1 teaspoon kosher salt
- 2 cups kale
- 2 teaspoons oregano
- 2 garlic cloves
- 1 red bell pepper
- Half of an onion
- 2 tablespoons olive oil

COOK TIME: 50 mins
SERVING: 6

INSTRUCTIONS

1. Preheat oven to 400 degrees Fahrenheit.
2. Heat the oil in a large oven-safe skillet over medium heat.
3. Toss in the onion.
4. Cook for 5 minutes, or until the vegetables are tender.
5. Combine the garlic, red pepper, kale, oregano, red pepper flakes, and salt in a large mixing bowl after 5 minutes of sautéing.
6. Add the tomato paste to the pan 1–2 minutes of sautéing.
7. Combine the chickpeas, canned tomatoes, orzo, and broth in a large mixing bowl.
8. Bring to a low boil, then reduce to low heat.
9. Bake until the orzo is tender, about 10-15 minutes.
10. Finish by adding the butter and crumbling the feta over the top.

Tip: If you want the feta to soften, crumble it and return it to the oven for about 5 minutes before serving.

GREEK WALNUT CAKE

INGREDIENTS

- **For the Cake**
- ¼ teaspoon salt
- 1 cup of walnuts
- 1 teaspoon ground cinnamon
- 1 ½ cups all-purpose flour
- 3 teaspoons baking powder
- 1 teaspoon of baking soda
- ½ teaspoon of vanilla extract
- ¾ cup milk warmed
- 1½ cups sugar
- 5 eggs room temperature
- ¾ cup butter
- **For the Syrup**
- 1 cinnamon stick
- ¼ teaspoon whole cloves
- 2 cups sugar
- Zest of one lemon
- 2 cups water

COOK TIME: *30 mins*
SERVING: *20*

INSTRUCTIONS

1. Preheat the oven to 350 degrees Fahrenheit.
2. Set aside a medium-sized bowl containing cinnamon, flour, and salt.
3. Using a mixer, beat the sugar and butter until light and fluffy, scraping down the sides of the bowl as needed.
4. Mix the eggs one at a time until well combined, then add the vanilla.
5. Mix the heated milk, baking powder, and baking soda carefully.
6. While the mixer is low, add the dry ingredients and mix until they are thoroughly combined.
7. Mix in the chopped walnuts.
8. Bake for half an hour after pouring the batter onto a buttered pan.
9. Combine all syrup ingredients in a small saucepan and bring to a boil.
10. Remove the cake from the oven once it is done.
11. Add the syrup carefully and serve.

GREK MEATBALLS

INGREDIENTS

- **Meatballs**
- ¾ teaspoon salt
- Black pepper to taste
- ½ teaspoon oregano
- 1 tablespoon olive oil
- ¼ cup fresh parsley
- 6 large mint leaves
- 60g panko breadcrumbs
- 1 egg
- 6.5oz. pork mince
- 2 garlic cloves, minced
- 1 lb. beef mince
- 1 red onion
- **Cooking**
- Finely chopped parsley
- Greek yogurt
- 3 tablespoons olive oil
- ½ cup flour

COOK TIME: 32 mins
SERVING: 5

INSTRUCTIONS

1. Put the onions into a large mixing bowl, then add the rest of the Meatball components.
2. Mix well with your hands for a few seconds.
3. Add heaping tablespoons of the mixture onto a work surface.
4. After that, roll into balls.
5. Heat the oil over medium-high heat in a large skillet.
6. Place the meatballs in the pan after lightly dredging them in flour.
7. Cook for 6 minutes after rolling them around.
8. Remove the meatballs to a platter, cover to keep warm, and continue with the remaining meatballs.
9. Serve as a starter with pita bread and tzatziki as part of a mezze plate.

STUFFED GRAPE LEAVES

INGREDIENTS

- About 4 cups chicken broth
- Juice of 2 lemons
- ½ cup fresh parsley
- 2 tomatoes
- 1 teaspoon allspice
- ½ teaspoon cumin
- Kosher salt
- Black pepper
- 1 large yellow onion
- 12 oz. lean ground beef
- 1 ½ cup short grain rice
- Extra virgin olive oil
- 1 16-oz jar grape leaves in brine

COOK TIME: 95 mins
SERVING: 15

INSTRUCTIONS

1. Soak the rice in a large bowl of water for many hours.
2. Cook the meat while the rice is being soaked.
3. Heat 1 tablespoon olive oil in a large skillet.
4. Cook for a few minutes after adding the onions.
5. Cook until the meat is completely browned.
6. Season meat with pepper, kosher salt, and spices.
7. Toss everything together.
8. Mix the drained rice, meat, and fresh herbs in a mixing dish.
9. Lightly season with kosher salt.
10. Lightly brush the bottom of a large cooking pot with extra virgin olive oil.
11. At the bottom, arrange a few grape leaves.
12. Serve with sliced tomatoes on top.
13. Place 1 heaping spoonful of filling in the center of each leaf, then roll it up.
14. Bring the broth or water to a boil before pouring it over the grape leaves.
15. Cover the saucepan with the lid and cook for half an hour over moderate flame.
16. Serve with lemon wedges and a serving of Greek Tzatziki sauce or plain yogurt.

MOUSSAKA

INGREDIENTS

- ½ tablespoon soft sugar
- 550g potatoes
- 400g can tomatoes
- 2 tablespoons tomato purée
- 2 bay leaves
- 200ml red wine
- 3 heaped teaspoon oregano
- 2 teaspoons ground cinnamon
- 1 onion
- 2 fat garlic cloves
- 3 medium aubergines
- 800g lamb mince
- 6 tablespoons olive oil
- **For the Béchamel Sauce**
- the whole nutmeg for grating
- 1 large egg
- 40g unsalted butter
- 40g parmesan

INSTRUCTIONS

1. Heat the oil over high heat in a frying pan.
2. Drizzle 4 tablespoons of oil over the aubergine slices and cook them.
3. Heat 1 tablespoon of the oil in a medium-high-heat saucepan.
4. Cook for 8-10 minutes after adding the mince.
5. Place in a mixing dish and put aside.
6. Fill the casserole with the remaining oil.
7. Add the onion and a sprinkle of salt to the pan.
8. Cook for another minute after adding the cinnamon, oregano, garlic, chili, and bay.
9. Pour the red wine into the pan with the lamb.
10. Combine the tomato purée, tomatoes, and brown sugar, as well as 200ml water, in a mixing bowl.
11. Reduce the heat to a low setting and continue to cook gradually.
12. Preheat the oven to 200 degrees Celsius.
13. Bring a big pot of water to a boil, lightly salted.
14. Cook for 6 minutes after adding the potato slices.

- 40g plain flour
- 450ml whole milk

COOK TIME: 2 hours
SERVING: 8

15. In a small saucepan, melt the butter, then add the flour, milk, salt, nutmeg, parmesan, and the entire egg, as well as the yolk.
16. Take a big rectangular ovenproof dish and line it with parchment paper.
17. Spoon one third of the meat into the dish and equally distribute it, followed by a layer of eggplant and potato, then the remaining meat and another layer of aubergines.
18. Finish with the béchamel and a palette knife to smooth the top.
19. Cook for half an hour, or until deep nicely browned, in the center of the oven.
20. Allow cooling for 10 minutes before serving.

GREK STUFFED PEPPERS

INGREDIENTS

- 6 bell peppers
- ¾ cup chicken broth
- ¼ cup tomato sauce
- 2 ¼ cup water
- 1 cup white rice
- ¾ teaspoon hot paprika
- 1 cup chickpeas
- 1 small bunch of parsley
- 1 teaspoon ground allspice
- 2 garlic cloves
- ½ lb. ground beef
- Kosher salt + black pepper
- 1 small yellow onion
- Greek olive oil

COOK TIME: 65 mins
SERVING: 6

INSTRUCTIONS

1. Heat one tablespoon extra-virgin oil in a medium heavy saucepan.
2. Cook the onions until they are golden brown.
3. Cook the beef over medium-high heat at this point.
4. Add allspice, pepper, salt, and garlic to taste.
5. Cook for a few minutes after adding the chickpeas.
6. Cook the rice after adding it.
7. Add the paprika, parsley, and tomato sauce to the same saucepan.
8. To blend, stir everything together.
9. Bring the water to a boil, then reduce to low heat.
10. Preheat the grill to medium-high while the rice is being cooked.
11. For 10-15 minutes, grill the bell peppers.
12. Preheat oven to 350 degrees Fahrenheit.
13. Fill stuffed peppers with a third of a cup of broth or water.
14. Fill each bell pepper with the prepared rice, pork, and chickpeas filling mixture.
15. Bake for 30 minutes, covered.
16. Serve with parsley as a garnish.

GREEK BEAN SOUP (FESOLADA)

INGREDIENTS

- A pinch of paprika
- Salt and freshly ground pepper
- 130ml extra virgin olive oil
- 2 tablespoons tomato paste
- 1 large white onion
- 3 stalks of celery
- 4 carrots
- 500g dry kidney beans

COOK TIME: *90 mins*
SERVING: *6*

INSTRUCTIONS

1. Place the beans in a pot with enough cold water to cover them to make the fasolada.
2. Bring to a boil, reduce to low heat and continue to parboil for 35 minutes.
3. Chop the celery, onion, and carrots finely.
4. Heat 4 tablespoons of olive oil in a deep pan, then add the chopped veggies and combine.
5. Sauté for 2 minutes, add the tomato paste and cook for another minute.
6. Pour enough hot water to cover the parboiled beans plus a little bit more into the pan and mix softly.
7. Simmer the fasolada for around 35 minutes with the cover on.
8. Season with salt and pepper and drizzle with the leftover olive oil.
9. Cook for a few minutes longer.
10. Serve with a few Kalamata olives while they are still hot.

GREEK PITA BREAD

INGREDIENTS

- 1.5 tablespoon sugar
- 1.5 tablespoon table salt
- 4 tablespoons extra-virgin olive oil
- 0.25 oz. dry yeast
- 2 cups water
- 5.75 cups bread flour

COOK TIME: 3 hours
SERVING: 16

INSTRUCTIONS

1. Fill a bowl halfway with lukewarm water, then add and dissolve the dried yeast and sugar.
2. Add half of the flour to the mixing bowl, toss to combine, and add the salt and extra-virgin olive oil.
3. Knead the dough until it is smooth and elastic, about 10 minutes.
4. Now divide the Pita dough into 24 sections.
5. Grease the bottom of the skillet and place it over medium heat.
6. Make a circle out of the first dough ball.
7. Place the Pita on the heated skillet and cook for approximately 1 minute per side.

Tip: If not serving right away, seal the Pitas in a plastic bag and keep them in the fridge for up to two days.

GREEK GREEN BEANS

INGREDIENTS

- 2 teaspoons sugar
- Salt to taste
- 2 pounds green beans
- 3 large tomatoes
- 2 cups onions
- 1 clove garlic
- ¾ cup olive oil

COOK TIME: 75 mins
SERVING: 8

INSTRUCTIONS

1. Heat the olive oil over moderate flame in a large skillet.
2. In a pan, cook and sauté the onions and garlic until soft.
3. Combine the sugar, tomatoes, green beans, and salt in a pan.
4. Reduce to low heat and simmer for another 45 minutes, or until the beans are tender.
5. Serve hot with rice.

GREEK SALAD

INGREDIENTS

- 85g feta cheese
- 4 tablespoons Greek olive oil
- 16 Kalamata olives
- 1 teaspoon dried oregano
- 1 cucumber
- ½ a red onion
- 4 large vine tomatoes

COOK TIME: 15 *mins*
SERVING: 4

INSTRUCTIONS

1. Combine feta cheese chunks, oregano, Kalamata olives, red onion, cucumber, tomatoes, and Greek extra virgin olive oil in a large mixing bowl.
2. Season lightly, then serve with crusty bread to soak up the juices.

GREEK FETA DIP

INGREDIENTS

- 1 Persian cucumber
- 1 Roma tomato
- 2 tablespoons dill
- 2 tablespoons parsley leaves
- 1 clove garlic
- ¼ cup pepperoncini peppers
- 1 tablespoon lemon juice
- 2 teaspoons lemon zest
- 4 ounces cream cheese
- 1 cup Greek yogurt
- 8 ounces feta

COOK TIME: 15 mins
SERVING: 8

INSTRUCTIONS

1. Beat lemon zest, lemon juice, yogurt, cream cheese, feta, and garlic in the bowl of an electric mixer, on medium speed until light and frothy for about 60 seconds.
2. Add dill, pepperoncini peppers, and parsley in the end.
3. Refrigerate for up to two days after covering.
4. Serve with cucumber and tomato on the side, if preferred.

CHICKEN SOUVLAKI

INGREDIENTS

- ½ teaspoon salt
- 1 ½ pounds chicken breast
- 2 cloves garlic
- 1 teaspoon oregano
- 2 tablespoons lemon juice
- ¼ cup olive oil
- **Sauce**
- 1 pinch salt
- 6 wooden skewers
- 2 teaspoons white vinegar
- 1 clove garlic
- ½ cucumber
- 1 tablespoon olive oil
- 1 (6 ounces) Greek-style yogurt

COOK TIME: 2.5 hours
SERVING: 6

INSTRUCTIONS

1. Combine oregano, garlic, cloves, lemon juice, olive oil, and salt in a large re-sealable bag.
2. Add the chicken and toss it in the marinade.
3. Refrigerate for three hours to marinate.
4. Combine the garlic, vinegar, olive oil, cucumber, yogurt, and salt in a bowl.
5. Optional: You can put Tzatziki in refrigerator to allow flavors to meld.
6. Preheat an outside grill over medium-high heat and brush the grate liberally with oil.
7. Soak wooden skewers for fifteen minutes in a dish of water.
8. Remove the chicken from the marinade and thread it onto the skewers that have been soaked.
9. Cook the skewers for around 8 minutes per side on a hot grill.
10. Serve with tzatziki sauce on the side.

GREEK BAKLAVA

INGREDIENTS

- 1 teaspoon vanilla extract
- ½ cup honey
- 1 cup water
- 1 cup white sugar
- 1 cup butter
- 1 teaspoon cinnamon
- 1 pound chopped nuts
- 1 (16 ounces) phyllo dough

COOK TIME: 60 mins
SERVING: 6

INSTRUCTIONS

1. Preheat the oven to 350 degrees Fahrenheit.
2. Butter the pan's bottom and sides.
3. Toss nuts with cinnamon once they are chopped. Set aside.
4. Roll out the phyllo dough.
5. Butter two sheets of dough and place them in the pan.
6. Continue layering sheets until you have a total of eight.
7. Add 3 teaspoons of the nut mixture on top.
8. Add nuts, butter, and two sheets of dough to the top.
9. Cut square or rectangular shapes all the way down to the bottom of the skillet using a sharp knife.
10. Brown and crisp the baklava for 50 minutes in the oven.
11. Bring sugar and water to a boil until the sugar melts.
12. Mix in the vanilla and honey.
13. Cook for around 20 minutes on low heat.
14. Remove the baklava from the oven and pour the sweet sauce over it immediately.
15. Allow cooling.
16. Use cupcake sheets for serving.

GREEK CHICKPEA SOUP

INGREDIENTS

- 2 tablespoons flour
- Vegetable stock (optional)
- Salt and pepper
- Juice of 2 lemons
- 1 bay leaf
- 2 teaspoons dried oregano
- 1 large red onion
- ½ a cup olive oil
- 500g dry chickpeas

COOK TIME: 2 *hours*
SERVING: 5

INSTRUCTIONS

1. Fill a big pan halfway with cold water and add the chickpeas.
2. Increase the heat to high and bring it to a boil.
3. Drain the chickpeas, then return them to the pan with enough heated water to cover them completely.
4. Add the oregano, onion, olive oil, and bay leaves to the pot and brings to a boil.
5. Reduce the heat to low heat and cover the pot.
6. Allow for 1-2 hours of cooking time.
7. Towards the end of the cooking time, mix the flour and lemon juice in a bowl, then gently pour in 1-2 ladles of the soup.
8. Season with salt and pepper as you carefully pour the mixture into the pan with the chickpeas.
9. Stir the soup gradually for 2-3 minutes or until it thickens.
10. This Greek chickpea soup tastes delicious when served hot.

TIROPITA

INGREDIENTS

- ½ lb. phyllo dough
- ½ lb. unsalted butter
- 3 eggs, beaten
- ½ teaspoon. salt
- ½ lb. cottage cheese
- ½ lb. feta cheese

COOK TIME: 50 mins
SERVING: 6

INSTRUCTIONS

1. In a mixing dish, combine the eggs, cheeses, and salt.
2. Stir until everything is well combined.
3. On your cutting board, lay one sheet of phyllo horizontally.
4. Brush with butter.
5. At the end of each strip, place one spoonful of the cheese mixture.
6. To form a triangle, fold the corner over.
7. Place on the pan that has been prepared.
8. Butter the tops of the rolls.
9. Preheat oven to 350°F and bake for 10 to 15 minutes, or until golden brown.
10. Allow cooling for a few minutes before serving.

Tip: If you want to prepare these ahead of time, freeze the unbaked tiropitas. Freeze the tiropitas in a single layer and then transfer them to a Ziploc bag.

GREEK EGGPLANT DIP

INGREDIENTS

- Kalamata olives (optional)
- Feta cheese (garnish)
- 1 lemon
- ¼ cup olive oil
- Kosher salt and black pepper
- ½ teaspoon cumin
- ½ teaspoon pepper flakes
- ¼ red onion
- 2 large garlic cloves
- 1 cup parsley
- 2 large eggplants

COOK TIME: 20 mins
SERVING: 6

INSTRUCTIONS

1. Place the eggplant on a grill and cook it over a gas flame.
2. Set the eggplant aside in a bowl until it is cold enough to handle.
3. Place the eggplant in a large mixing dish.
4. Combine the lemon juice, parsley, onion, garlic, and olive oil in a mixing bowl.
5. Season with salt, pepper, and spices as desired.
6. Stir everything together to blend.
7. Place the eggplant dip on a serving platter and spread it out evenly.
8. Drizzle extra virgin olive oil over the dish.
9. Serve with crusty bread or pita bread.

Tip: To blitz the eggplant with the rest of the ingredients, you may use a food processor. However, don't go overboard, or you will end up with a sloppy mess.

GREEK ORANGE CAKE

INGREDIENTS

- **Syrup**
- 1 teaspoon cinnamon
- 1 orange
- 1 ½ cups water
- 2 cups white sugar
- **Cake**
- ½ cup white sugar
- 1 tablespoon baking powder
- 1 (7 ounces) Greek yogurt
- ¾ cup olive oil
- 3 oranges
- 5 eggs
- 1 (16 ounces) phyllo dough

COOK TIME: 2 hours
SERVING: 12

INSTRUCTIONS

1. Put two cups of water, sugar, and cinnamon in a pan over medium heat.
2. Squeeze in the orange juice and toss in the half-juiced oranges.
3. Bring to a boil and cook for 8 minutes on high heat.
4. Remove the pan from the heat.
5. Preheat oven to 375 Fahrenheit.
6. Remove the phyllo sheets from the packaging and set them aside.
7. Slice one orange.
8. Juice and zest the remaining oranges.
9. Combine the sugar, olive oil, yogurt, eggs, orange zest, orange juice, and baking powder in a blender or food processor.
10. Combine all ingredients in a high-powered blender until frothy.
11. Pour the orange and egg mix over the shred phyllo on the baking pan.
12. Bake for 45 minutes in a preheated oven.
13. Remove the cake from the oven and pour the cooled syrup over it right away.
14. Serve by slicing into squares.

GREEK LENTIL SOUP

INGREDIENTS

- 1 teaspoon olive oil
- 1 teaspoon red wine vinegar
- 1 tablespoon tomato paste
- Salt and ground black pepper
- 1 pinch rosemary
- 2 bay leaves
- 1-quart water
- 1 pinch oregano
- 1 medium onion
- 1 large carrot
- ¼ cup olive oil
- 1 tablespoon garlic
- 8 ounces brown lentils

COOK TIME: 80 mins
SERVING: 4

INSTRUCTIONS

1. Combine the lentils and enough water to cover them in a large saucepan.
2. Bring a pot of water to a boil, then simmer for 10 minutes before draining.
3. In a medium saucepan, heat the olive oil.
4. Cook and stir for 5 minutes after adding the onion, garlic, and carrot.
5. Combine the rosemary, oregano, water, lentils, and bay leaves in a large mixing bowl.
6. Bring the water to a boil. Reduce to low heat, cover, cook, and stir.
7. Season with salt and pepper after adding the tomato paste.
8. Cover and cook for 30 minutes, stirring regularly.
9. If the soup becomes too thick, add more water.
10. Add olive oil and red wine vinegar, to taste and serve.

FASOLATHA

INGREDIENTS

- Salt to taste
- Ground black pepper to taste
- 3 cups water
- 2 tablespoons parsley
- 1 teaspoon dried thyme
- ½ cup olive oil
- 1 tablespoon tomato paste
- 1 teaspoon dried oregano
- 1 stalk celery
- 1 (14.5 ounces) tomatoes
- 1 onion
- 2 small carrots
- 1 cup white kidney beans

COOK TIME: 60 mins
SERVING: 6

INSTRUCTIONS

1. Fill a big saucepan halfway with water and add the beans.
2. Allow 2–3 minutes to boil.
3. Bring 3 cups of water to a boil over the beans.
4. In a large mixing bowl, combine the olive oil, thyme, oregano, tomato paste, tomatoes, onions, celery, carrots, and salt and pepper.
5. Cook until the beans are tender for about 50 - 70 minutes.
6. Toss the parsley together.
7. Cook all ingredients except parsley for approximately 3 minutes under fifteen pounds' pressure if using a pressure cooker.
8. Add the parsley and mix well.

LOUKOUMADES

INGREDIENTS

- 4 cups vegetable oil
- 2 teaspoons cinnamon
- ½ cup honey
- ½ cup water
- 3 eggs
- 4 cups all-purpose flour
- 1 teaspoon salt
- ⅓ cup butter
- ½ cup warm milk
- ¼ cup white sugar
- 1 cup warm water
- 2 (.25 ounce) active dry yeast

COOK TIME: 90 mins
SERVING: 25

INSTRUCTIONS

1. Spread the yeast over the heated water in a small dish.
2. Allow to sit for 5 minutes or until the yeast softens and forms a creamy foam.
3. Combine the heated milk, salt, and sugar in a large mixing bowl and stir to dissolve.
4. Stir the yeast mixture into the milk mixture to incorporate it.
5. Mix the eggs, butter, and flour until the dough is smooth and soft.
6. Allow 30 minutes to cover the bowl.
7. Combine honey and water in a saucepan and boil over medium-high heat.
8. Remove the honey syrup from the heat and set it aside to cool.
9. In a deep-fryer, heat the oil to 375 degrees F.
10. In batches, drop the dough pieces into the heated oil.
11. Fry till golden brown on the bottom, then flip and fry the other side for two or three minutes per batch in the hot oil.
12. Drizzle with honey syrup and cinnamon before placing on a baking pan.
13. Warm the dish before serving.

GREEK LEMON POTATOES

INGREDIENTS

- ½ teaspoon black pepper
- 3 cups chicken broth
- 2 teaspoons salt
- 1 teaspoon oregano
- ⅓ cup olive oil
- 2 lemons, juiced
- 3 pounds potatoes

COOK TIME: 75 mins
SERVING: 6

INSTRUCTIONS

1. Preheat the oven to 400 degrees Fahrenheit.
2. Place the potato wedges in a large mixing bowl.
3. Toss the wedges in olive oil and lemon juice to coat them.
4. Toss potatoes again with oregano, salt, and black pepper to coat.
5. Arrange potato wedges in a thin layer in a 2-inch-deep pan.
6. Pour chicken stock over the potatoes.
7. In a preheated oven, roast potatoes until soft and nicely browned for one hour.
8. Serve immediately.

GREEK LEMON CHICKEN SOUP

INGREDIENTS

- 16 lemons
- 8 egg yolks
- 1 cup white rice
- 1 cup chicken meat
- ¼ cup margarine
- ¼ cup all-purpose flour
- 6 tablespoons chicken soup base
- ¼ teaspoon white pepper
- ½ cup onion
- ½ cup celery
- ½ cup lemon juice
- ½ cup carrots
- 8 cups chicken broth

COOK TIME: 65 mins
SERVING: 16

INSTRUCTIONS

1. Mix the soup base, chicken stock, celery, onions, carrots, lemon juice, and white pepper in a big saucepan.
2. Bring to a boil over high heat, then reduce to low heat and cook for 20 minutes.
3. Combine the butter and flour in a mixing bowl.
4. After that, gently include it into the soup mixture.
5. Cook for another 10 minutes.
6. In the meantime, whisk the egg yolks until they are light in color.
7. Gradually drizzle part of the heated soup into the egg yolks while continually swirling.
8. Return the egg mixture to the soup pot and heat until it is fully cooked.
9. Combine the rice and chicken in a large mixing bowl.
10.
    erve the heated soup in dishes with lemon slices on top.

.

CHICKEN GYROS

INGREDIENTS

- 2 lb. chicken thigh fillets
- **Tzatziki**
- ¼ teaspoon salt
- Black pepper
- 1 tablespoon extra-virgin olive oil
- 1 garlic clove
- 1 ¼ cups Greek yogurt
- 1 tablespoon lemon juice
- **Marinade**
- 1 teaspoon salt
- Black pepper
- 3 tablespoons Greek yogurt
- 1 ½ tablespoon oregano
- 3 tablespoons lemon juice
- 1 tablespoon olive oil
- 1 tbsp white wine vinegar
- 3 garlic cloves
- 2 cucumbers
- **Salad**
- ¼ cup parsley leaves
- Salt and pepper
- 3 cucumbers
- ½ red Spanish onion
- 3 tomatoes

COOK TIME: 26 mins
SERVING: 4

INSTRUCTIONS

1. Combine the marinade ingredients in a Ziploc bag and massage to combine with the chicken.
2. In a bowl, place the cucumber.
3. Toss in the tzatziki ingredients and stir to incorporate.
4. Allow at least twenty minutes to rest.
5. Combine all the salad ingredients in a mixing dish and put them aside.
6. Preheat the grill on medium-high heat after brushing it with oil.
7. Cook marinated chicken for 2–3 minutes on each side, or until lightly browned and cooked throughout.
8. Take the chicken out of the grill and set it aside.
9. Add salad in the center of the pita (optional), then chicken and Tzatziki should go on top.

Tip: If the chicken thighs are bigger, you may need to split them in half.

GREEK BUTTER COOKIES

INGREDIENTS

- 2 ¼ cups all-purpose flour
- ½ cup confectioners' sugar
- ½ teaspoon vanilla extract
- ½ teaspoon almond extract
- ¾ cup white sugar
- 1 egg
- 1 cup butter

COOK TIME: 28 mins
SERVING: 40 cookies

INSTRUCTIONS

1. Preheat oven to 375 degrees Fahrenheit.
2. Oil the cookie sheets.
3. Cream the sugar, butter, and egg in a medium mixing bowl until smooth.
4. Combine the vanilla and almond extracts in a mixing bowl.
5. Mix in the flour to make a dough.
6. Roll roughly a teaspoon of dough into balls at a time.
7. Place cookies 2 inches apart on cookie sheets that have been prepped.
8. Bake for 10 minutes in a preheated oven or until gently browned and firm.
9. Before dusting with confectioners' sugar, let the cookies cool fully.

TZATZIKI

INGREDIENTS

- 1 medium clove garlic
- ½ teaspoon sea salt
- 2 tablespoons mint
- 1 tablespoon lemon juice
- 1 ½ cups plain Greek yogurt
- 2 tablespoons olive oil
- 2 cups cucumber

COOK TIME: 15 mins
SERVING: 2

INSTRUCTIONS

1. Place the sliced cucumber in a serving bowl once it is squeezed.
2. Stir together the garlic, lemon juice, herbs, olive oil, yogurt, and salt in a mixing dish.
3. Allow the flavors to mix for 5 minutes before serving.
4. Tzatziki can be served right away or refrigerated for later.

Tip: Tzatziki can be kept refrigerated for up to 4 days.

SPANOKOPITA

INGREDIENTS

- 8 sheets phyllo dough
- ¼ cup olive oil
- ½ cup ricotta cheese
- 1 cup feta cheese
- ½ cup fresh parsley
- 2 eggs
- 2 garlic cloves
- 2 lbs. spinach
- 1 large onion
- 1 bunch green onion
- 3 tablespoons olive oil

COOK TIME: 60 mins
SERVING: 8

INSTRUCTIONS

1. Preheat oven to 375 degrees Fahrenheit.
2. Heat 3 tablespoons of olive oil in a large pan over medium heat.
3. Sauté green onions, onion, and garlic until softened and gently browned.
4. Continue to sauté after adding the spinach and parsley.
5. Combine the ricotta, eggs, and feta in a medium mixing bowl.
6. Add the spinach mixture and stir well.
7. Brush 1 sheet of phyllo dough with olive oil and place in preheated baking pan.
8. Brush another layer of phyllo dough with olive oil and place on top.
9. Fold the greens and cheese mixture into the pan.
10. Bake for 30 minutes to an hour, until nicely browned, in a preheated oven.
11. Serve immediately after cutting into squares.

GREEK FRIED CHEESE

INGREDIENTS

- Oil for frying
- ½ lemon
- 50g plain flour
- 110g cheese (Graviera)

COOK TIME: 15 mins
SERVING: 1

INSTRUCTIONS

1. Slice a big cheese block to make this saganaki dish.
2. Dip the cheese in the flour, brushing off the excess flour if necessary.
3. Pour some oil into a large pan.
4. Add the cheese to the hot oil and fry for a few minutes on both ends.
5. Serve hot with this Greek cheese saganaki dish and top with lemon.

Tip: The saganaki will dissolve into the pan if the cheese is chopped thinner.

GREEK FRIES

INGREDIENTS

- 2 tablespoons red onion
- 4 lemon wedges
- ¼ cup feta crumbles
- 2 tablespoons parsley
- 1 tablespoon Greek Seasoning
- ½ teaspoon kosher salt
- 2 tablespoons olive oil
- 6 medium gold potatoes

COOK TIME: 30 mins
SERVING: 4

INSTRUCTIONS

1. Preheat the oven to 450 degrees Fahrenheit.
2. Slice the potatoes into fries in the meantime.
3. Soak fries for 10 minutes in cold water.
4. Toss the fries with Greek seasoning, olive oil, and kosher salt in a dry bowl.
5. Preheat the oven to 350°F and bake the fries for twenty minutes.
6. Take them out of the oven and turn gently.
7. Bake for another 10 to 15 minutes.
8. Place the fries on a serving plate and top with feta cheese crumbles.

Tip: The number of fries that can fit on two oven pans is 2 pounds; however, you can make more if necessary.

Chapter 2: Macedonian Recipes

North Macedonia, a real gem of a nation in the Balkan peninsula's middle, is a tiny and colorful country. The many antique monastic landmarks, scenic lakes, and appealing food will draw visitors to North Macedonia. The rich and bright traditional recipes, some of which date back generations, will conjure up several of the most delectable meals you will ever taste. Salads are popular among people before meals. Juicy meat combined with fresh organic veggies and served with various pastries and bread are other Macedonian favorites. Macedonians are recognized for their friendliness; thus, neighbors and friends are frequently invited over for a glass of rakija. Have a look at these delicious Macedonian recipes.

MACEDONIAN FISH WITH RICE

INGREDIENTS

- 2 handfuls rice
- Salt
- Pepper
- Paprika powder
- 1 medium onion
- 1 teaspoon vegetable stock powder
- 4 large chicken legs

COOK TIME: 50 mins
SERVING: 4

INSTRUCTIONS

1. Boil the chicken legs for around twenty minutes in salted water.
2. Meanwhile, dice the onions and cook them until they are transparent.
3. In a baking dish, place the uncooked rice.
4. Remove the cooked chicken legs from the water and lay them on top of the raw rice.
5. Arrange the fried onions on top of the rice.
6. Pour over it the water that the chicken legs were cooked in.
7. Add the pepper, vegetable stock, and paprika powder and mix well.
8. Preheat the oven to 180 degrees Celsius and bake the pan or tin until the rice has absorbed all water.
9. Serve hot.

MACEDONIAN KEBABS

INGREDIENTS

- **For the Kebapi**
- Onion (optional)
- Red pepper flakes (optional)
- ¼ cup hot water
- Wooden skewers
- 1 teaspoon black pepper
- ½ teaspoon baking soda
- 2 teaspoons red pepper flakes
- 2 teaspoons salt
- 2 teaspoons paprika
- 1 teaspoon cayenne pepper
- 4 garlic cloves
- 3 tablespoons parsley
- ½ pound lamb (ground)
- 1 small yellow onion
- ½ pound pork (ground)
- 1 pound beef (ground)

INSTRUCTIONS

1. Put the pork, beef, and lamb in a large mixing bowl and mix well.
2. Stir in the water and season with black pepper, salt, red pepper flakes, cayenne pepper, paprika, parsley, garlic, onion, and baking soda.
3. Refrigerate for 4 hours before serving.
4. Form the ground beef mixture into sausages by rolling it out.
5. Preheat the grill to medium-high temperature.
6. Grill kebapi for 10 to 12 minutes.
7. Place the kebapi on a serving plate.
8. Combine a tablespoon of paprika and red pepper flakes in a small dish.
9. While the kebapi is grilling, make the yogurt sauce by whisking together all ingredients in a single dish until fully combined.
10. Check for salt and adjust as needed.
11. Serve the kebapi with the paprika combination and sliced onions on the side.

- **For the Yogurt Sauce**
- 1 tablespoon lemon juice
- Salt, to taste
- 2 tablespoons olive oil
- 2 garlic cloves
- 1 cup plain yogurt

COOK TIME: 90 mins
SERVING: 12

MACEDONIAN TERRATOR

INGREDIENTS

- 1-liter plain yogurt
- 120ml double cream
- 1 tablespoon mint
- 1 teaspoon lemon juice
- 1 clove garlic
- 1 tablespoon dill
- 1 tablespoon sea salt flakes
- 2 cucumbers

COOK TIME: 30 mins
SERVING: 6

INSTRUCTIONS

1. Sprinkle the salt over the sliced cucumbers in a colander.
2. Set aside for twenty minutes to drain.
3. Combine the mint, dill, garlic, drained cucumbers, and lime juice in the bowl of a food processor, and whiz for thirty seconds.
4. Blitz for another thirty seconds, scraping down the sides with a spatula until you get a thin purée.
5. Stir the yogurt and cream into the cucumber combined with a spatula.
6. Chill for at least two hours before serving.
7. Ladle the chilled soup into dishes and top with cucumber slices and dill when ready to serve.

MACEDONIAN STYLE JUICY MEATBALLS

INGREDIENTS

- 1 tablespoon brandy
- Parsley
- Thyme
- 2 tablespoons breadcrumbs
- Black pepper
- 1 egg
- 1 cup beef
- 1 head onion
- 14 oz. pork

COOK TIME: 45 mins
SERVING: 4

INSTRUCTIONS

1. Finely chop the onions and parsley.
2. Put the meat through a meat grinder after cutting it into pieces.
3. In a mixing dish, combine it with the egg, spices, parsley, onions, and breadcrumbs.
4. Knead, add alcohol, and knead a meatball mince.
5. Make round meatballs of the same size.
6. In a deep skillet, heat the oil and add the meatballs.
7. Fry them on all sides until they are done, and a lovely brown color has developed.
8. Drain on paper towels after removing them from the pan.
9. Serve with fries and beer.

MACEDONIAN MACARONI

INGREDIENTS

- 1 teaspoon black pepper
- 2/3 cup Feta cheese
- 1 cup whole milk
- 4 cups Kashkaval cheese
- 2 tablespoons olive oil
- 6 eggs
- 1-pound bucatini pasta

COOK TIME: 60 mins
SERVING: 6

INSTRUCTIONS

1. Follow the package directions for cooking the pasta.
2. Spray a baking dish with nonstick cooking spray and add the spaghetti.
3. Whisk together the eggs and milk, then add the Kashkaval and black pepper.
4. Pour the sauce over the spaghetti and top with the Feta cheese.
5. Cover and bake for twenty minutes in a 350°F oven, then uncover and bake for another fifteen minutes, or until the eggs are set, and the pasta is slightly crispy on top.
6. Serve immediately.

MACEDONIAN EGGPLANT SALAD

INGREDIENTS

- 1 cucumber
- 2 scallions
- ½ teaspoon salt
- 2 tablespoons dry red wine
- 2 small eggplants
- 2 medium tomatoes
- Pepper
- 1 teaspoon basil
- 2 cloves garlic
- ¼ cup olive oil
- ¼ cup oil
- ½ teaspoon oregano
- 1 sweet red pepper
- 1 green pepper
- ½ cup wine vinegar
- **Marinade**
- Juice from 1 lemon

COOK TIME: 50 mins
SERVING: 2

INSTRUCTIONS

1. Peel and slice the eggplant and add salt to the slices.
2. Allow for a 10-minute rest period.
3. Broil until both sides are golden brown.
4. Make the marinade. Allow the eggplant to marinade.
5. Allow 2 hours to chill.
6. Cut the other veggies into tiny bits just before serving.
7. Combine the eggplant and toss well.
8. Serve right away.

Chapter 3: Recipes from Cyprus

With a population of little over 1 million people, Cyprus certainly punches above its weight in terms of history, religion, culture, and food. This eastern Mediterranean island is said to be the home of the goddess Aphrodite, and it boasts a rough coastline with sand or pebble beaches, rocky coasts, sunbaked plains, wooded mountains, and one of the world's greatest climates. It is no wonder that winemaking has been a major industry in Cyprus for millennia, given the island's hot, dry summers, moderate winters, and limitless sunshine. Cooks use locally available fresh foods such as cereals and legumes, fresh fruit, veggies, herbs, lean protein, fish, and olive oil, just as they do in neighboring Greece. Try making these quick recipes from Cyprus cuisine, and you will fall in love with the taste.

BEEF STIFADO

INGREDIENTS

- 2 x 400g cans tomatoes
- 150ml red wine
- 1 tablespoon tomato purée
- 1 tablespoon red wine vinegar
- Pinch of cloves
- 1 tablespoon oregano
- 3 tablespoons olive oil
- 1 kg stewing beef
- 1 cinnamon stick
- Pinch of allspice
- 4 garlic cloves
- 4 bay leaves
- Pinch of caster sugar
- 600g baby onions

COOK TIME: 2 hours
SERVING: 6

INSTRUCTIONS

1. Preheat the oven to 180 degrees Celsius.
2. Brown the meat in a casserole with 2 tablespoons of oil over medium-high heat.
3. Pour the remaining oil into the pan.
4. Add the onions to the pan after peeling them, and then sprinkle the sugar on top.
5. Allow five minutes of sizzling.
6. Cook for 1 minute more after adding the cloves, allspice, cinnamon stick, bay, garlic, and oregano.
7. Cook for another minute after adding the tomato purée, then add the steak and any remaining juices.
8. Stir to coat in the spicy onion mixture.
9. Toss in the diced tomatoes and red wine vinegar.
10. Season to taste with salt and whisk well.
11. Bring to a simmer, stir once more, then cover and place in the oven for 1 hour.
12. Serve immediately.

COUPES

INGREDIENTS

- 2 tablespoons olive oil
- ½ cup (75g) plain flour
- 400g fine cracked wheat
- **Filling**
- 4 cups canola oil
- Greek yogurt and dried mint
- ½ bunch parsley
- 1 teaspoon cinnamon
- 300g pork mince
- Zest and juice of 1 lemon
- 2 onions
- 1 garlic clove
- 2 tablespoons olive oil

COOK TIME: 30 mins
SERVING: 4

INSTRUCTIONS

1. Combine the wheat and oil in a large mixing bowl to prepare the dough; add the boiling water, and season with salt and pepper to taste.
2. Cover with plastic wrap and mix thoroughly.
3. Meanwhile, heat oil in a big saucepan over medium heat.
4. Simmer for 2-3 minutes with the onion and garlic before adding the mince and continuing to cook.
5. Turn off the heat and stir in the parsley, lemon juice, lemon zest, and cinnamon.
6. Season with salt and pepper and leave aside to cool.
7. After the wheat mixture is cooled, knead in the flour.
8. Make 50g balls out of the dough.
9. Heat the oil over medium-high heat in a large saucepan until it reaches 180°C.
10. Deep-fry koupes in batches for 3-5 minutes.
    Remove the pan from the heat. Serve with a dollop of yogurt on top while hot.

CYPRUS GYRO BURGER

INGREDIENTS

- 2 tablespoons olive oil
- 4 hamburger buns
- ½ red bell pepper
- 1 teaspoon kosher salt
- 1 tablespoon Urfa Biber
- 1 tablespoon butter
- ½ tablespoon coriander
- ½ tablespoon cumin
- 1 small sweet onion
- 1 ¼ teaspoon red pepper flakes
- 1 tsp. sumac
- 1 pound beef
- 1 red onion
- 1 teaspoon lemon juice
- 4 cloves garlic
- 1 tablespoon fresh dill
- 2 ½ teaspoon lemon juice
- 1 tablespoon olive oil
- 2 ¼ cup plain yogurt
- ¾ cup cucumber

COOK TIME: 70 mins
SERVING: 4

INSTRUCTIONS

1. Toss the strained yogurt with 2 ½ tablespoons lemon juice in a mixing bowl.
2. Add one tablespoon of olive oil gradually.
3. Combine the dill, garlic, and drained cucumbers in a mixing bowl.
4. Combine the sumac, red onion, and lemon juice in a mixing bowl.
5. Cover and store in the refrigerator.
6. Combine the ground beef, Urfa Biber, cumin, coriander, red pepper flakes, chopped onion, and butter in a mixing bowl.
7. Gently combine with your hands.
8. Blend the bell pepper until it is largely liquefied in a blender.
9. Mix in the bell pepper and kosher salt with the meat.
10. Form the meat into patties by dividing it into four equal halves.
11. Preheat an outside grill to high heat and brush the grate gently with oil.
12. Grill for 5 minutes on high and medium heat.
13. Place each burger on a bun and top with cucumber and yogurt tzatziki and the red onion and sumac mixture soaked in lemon.

CYPRIOT PASTITIO

INGREDIENTS

- **Meat Sauce**
- 2 cups ripe tomatoes
- 1 cup parsley
- Salt and black pepper
- ½ teaspoon cinnamon
- 1 onion
- 1/3 cup olive oil
- 500g ground pork
- **Other Ingredients**
- 1 tablespoon dried mint
- 1 egg white
- 1 tablespoon salt
- 1/3 cup halloumi cheese
- 1 packet of tubular pasta
- **Bechamel Sauce**
- ¼ cup grated halloumi
- ½ teaspoon nutmeg
- ¼ teaspoon cinnamon

INSTRUCTIONS

1. Bring water to a boil in a saucepan and season with salt.
2. Cook the pasta until it is al dente, as directed on the box.
3. Heat the olive oil in a sautéing pan and cook the onion until transparent.
4. Cook for several minutes after adding the ground beef.
5. Cook while tossing in the cinnamon, pepper, salt, and tomatoes.
6. Mix the ingredients for the Béchamel sauce.
7. Meanwhile, whisk the egg white and combine it with the pasta, a few tablespoons of halloumi, and the mint.
8. Layer half of the pasta in a baking pan.
9. Place the ground beef on top, then the remaining pasta.
10. Top the pasta with the Béchamel sauce and some grated halloumi, as well as some cinnamon.

- ½ cup halloumi
- 3 whole eggs and 1 yolk
- ½ teaspoon salt
- 70 grams olive oil
- 70 grams flour
- 1.3 liter milk

COOK TIME: *2 hours*
SERVING: *9*

CYPRIOT TALATOURI TZATZIKI

INGREDIENTS

- 3 tablespoons fresh mint
- A pinch of salt
- 500g Greek yogurt
- Juice of 1 lemon
- 2 cloves of garlic
- ¼ of a cup olive oil
- 1 cucumber

COOK TIME: 10 mins
SERVING: 3 cups

INSTRUCTIONS

1. Pour salt and pepper on the cucumber and set it aside for 10 minutes.
2. Combine the garlic, cucumber, yogurt, mint, 1 lemon juice, olive oil, and a sprinkle of salt in a mixing bowl and blend until smooth.
3. Keep refrigerated and serve chilled.

CYPRIOT RICE AND LEMON STEW WITH SPINACH

INGREDIENTS

- 80 grams Arborio rice
- 700 ml water
- 1-piece bay leaves
- 15 ml red vinegar
- 30 grams tomato paste
- 1 piece vegetable stock cube
- 2 grams oregano
- 2 grams cumin powder
- 200 grams spinach
- 400 grams lentils
- 2 tablespoons olive oil
- 0.5 tsp salt
- 2 garlic cloves
- 40 grams kalamata olives
- 1 piece carrot
- 1 white onion
- **Garnish**
- 1 tablespoon olive oil
- 20 grams crispy onions
- 1 piece lemon
- 2 pieces of pitta bread

INSTRUCTIONS

1. Heat a big pan or pot over medium-low heat using a very good drizzle of olive oil.
2. Fry the olives, onion, and carrot with a bit of salt after the pan is heated.
3. Fry the oregano, garlic, and cumin after the onions are tender.
4. Simmer, covered, for 18-20 minutes with the vinegar, rice, measured water, bay leaves, stock cube, tomato paste, and lentils.
5. In the meantime, warm the pita pockets in the oven.
6. Stir in the spinach and cook for another four minutes, stirring periodically.
7. You can use lemon juice and salt to season the dish.
8. Drizzle with olive oil before serving.

COOK TIME: 40 mins
SERVING: 2

171

Chapter 4: Cretan Recipes

The Seven Countries Study, which found Cretans to have the best health conditions and lower rates of cardiovascular disease and cancer risk, has linked Cretan food to health since the early 1960s. Cretan food is flavorful, although it is not particularly diverse in ingredients. The flavorful outcome is obtained by the art of processing simple resources in Crete's traditional recipes, which may be prepared with only a few ingredients. Now that we've introduced Cretan food health benefits, it is time for you to gain a practical understanding of this unique food. We have compiled a list of our favorite Cretan dishes that you must try.

CRETAN MEAT PIE

INGREDIENTS

- ¼ cup olive oil
- 4 cups flour
- 9g dried yeast (one packet)
- 1 dash salt
- 1 cup warm water
- **Filling**
- 1 egg yolk, beaten
- 2 tablespoons sesame seeds
- ¼ cup meat juice
- Salt, pepper to taste
- 1 dash cinnamon
- ½ teaspoon oregano
- 350g mizithra cheese
- 20 leaves mint
- 600g lamb (small chunks)

INSTRUCTIONS

1. Combine the water and yeast in a large mixing bowl.
2. Combine the salt and oil in a mixing bowl.
3. Mix this into the water and add around 3 cups of flour to make the dough.
4. Allow the dough to rise slightly before transferring it to the baking dish.
5. Shape the dough.
6. Season the dough to taste with pepper, salt, and oregano.
7. Evenly distribute the meat bits on top.
8. Distribute the mizithra over the meat, ensuring equally distributed throughout the pie.
9. Place the mint leaves on top of the cheese.
10. With the remaining dough, roll out another sheet of pastry.
11. Brush the beaten egg all over the pie and sprinkle sesame seeds on top.
12. Preheat the oven to 350°F and bake the pie for half an hour.

COOK TIME: 40 mins
SERVING: 6

CRETAN WEDDING RISOTTO

INGREDIENTS

- 3 tablespoons (60 ml) lemon juice
- 1 tablespoon lemon zest
- 2 shallots
- 1½ cups Arborio rice
- 6 cups chicken stock
- 2 tablespoons (40 ml) ghee
- ½ teaspoon pepper
- 6 pieces of chicken
- 1 teaspoon salt
- 1 ½ tablespoon olive oil

COOK TIME: 35 mins
SERVING: 6

INSTRUCTIONS

1. Heat the olive oil in an oven-safe pan.
2. Rub the chicken with salt and pepper.
3. Place the chicken skin-side down in the pan and cook until golden and crispy.
4. Continue to cook on the other side.
5. Cover and continue to simmer with 1 ½ cup chicken stock.
6. Meanwhile, heat the oil in a separate skillet.
7. Fry the shallots until they are transparent.
8. Toss in the rice and toast it, rotating it to coat it with oil.
9. Slowly pour in the remaining chicken stock, constantly stirring until it is absorbed into the rice.
10. Whisk in the lemon juice and zest when the stock is entirely absorbed.
11. Place the rice on a platter.
12. Serve with cooked chicken on top.

BOUREKI

INGREDIENTS

- ½ cup flour
- ¼ cup water
- 2 tablespoons mint
- Salt and pepper
- 1 lb. ricotta cheese
- ½ lb. mizithra cheese
- ¾ cup olive oil
- 5 garlic cloves
- 2 lbs. large potatoes
- 1 large onion
- 3 lbs. large zucchini

COOK TIME: 90 mins
SERVING: 6

INSTRUCTIONS

1. Preheat oven to 375 degrees Fahrenheit.
2. Toss the potato, zucchini, and onion pieces in a deep bowl with salt, flour, and pepper to taste, all of the olive oil, garlic, mint, and grated cheese.
3. Fill a baking dish halfway with this mixture.
4. Add ¼ cup water carefully over the top
5. Preheat oven to 350°F and bake for 1 hour and fifteen minutes.
6. Allow 15 minutes for cooling before cutting into.
7. Serve right away.

CRETAN POTATOES

INGREDIENTS

- 6 tablespoons cream
- 2 tablespoons cmayonnaise
- Pepper & salt
- 500g sour cream
- Garlic
- 1 tablespoon olive oil
- 600g potatoes

COOK TIME: 90 mins
SERVING: 3

INSTRUCTIONS

1. Preheat the oven to 200 degrees Celsius.
2. Peel and slice the potatoes.
3. Cut and fry the garlic into a casserole dish with oil.
4. Season the Cretan potatoes using salt and pepper.
5. Combine the cream, sour cream, and mayonnaise in a mixing bowl.
6. Fill the casserole dish halfway with Cretan potatoes.
7. Bake for half an hour on the center shelf.

Tip: Cretan potatoes taste great with lamb steaks as a side dish.

CRETAN TOMATO SALAD

INGREDIENTS

- 200g feta, crumbled
- 2 handfuls of black olives
- 6 small oreganos
- 300g krisprolls
- 4 tablespoons olive oil
- 1 teaspoon dried oregano
- 4 tablespoons red wine vinegar
- 1.5kg beef tomatoes

COOK TIME: 20 mins
SERVING: 4

INSTRUCTIONS

1. Slice the tomatoes in halves.
2. Grate each tomato coarsely.
3. Combine the herbs, olive oil, vinegar, and spice to taste in a mixing bowl.
4. Crumble the krisprolls/rusks coarsely into bowls or plates, then top with the tomato mixture.
5. Serve with the feta and olives on top, drizzled with the remaining oil.

CRETAN CHEESE PIE WITH THYME AND HONEY

INGREDIENTS

- **For the Phyllo**
- 3¾ cups all-purpose flour
- ½ teaspoon kosher salt
- 1 tablespoon white vinegar
- 3 tablespoons olive oil
- **For the Filling**
- 1 tablespoon white sesame seeds
- Thyme honey, for serving
- 1 large egg
- 1 tablespoon black sesame seeds
- 5 oz. Tirumala cheese
- 1 teaspoon mint
- 12 oz. mizithra cheese

INSTRUCTIONS

1. Mix the olive oil, cold water, and vinegar in a small bowl.
2. Combine the flour and salt in a mixing dish.
3. Sprinkle the wet ingredients with the flour into the blender until the dough is tight and smooth.
4. Combine the cheeses, mint, and pulse until well blended in the bowl of a food processor.
5. Preheat oven to 375 degrees Fahrenheit.
6. Set aside one egg that is beaten with 1 teaspoon water in a small bowl.
7. Fill each pie with 1 heaping spoonful of filling and then seal.
8. Arrange the pies on the prepared baking pans, equally spaced.
9. After brushing the tops and sides with the egg wash, scatter the sesame seeds on top.
10. Bake until golden brown, about 30 minutes.
11. Warm the dish before serving.

COOK TIME: 2 hours
SERVING: 20

Chapter 5: Aegean Islands Recipes

The Aegean Sea, home to innumerable small and large islands with cuisine traditions dating back to Homer, conjures up idyllic visions of Greece. Islanders have a distinct existence characterized by a strong sense of place and familial ties. Aegean cooking can be viewed as a whole, shaped by the peculiarities of island life, isolation, and the harsh arid landscape that characterizes most Aegean islands. The basic ingredients were traditionally limited to a few garden veggies, lentils, forest greens, fish, and some meat, usually goat or lamb. But, over time, this modest list of raw materials grew into a plethora of delectable meals, odes to the resourcefulness of simple cooks who value one thing above all else: a reverence for great, seasonal foods. Make the flavorful dishes from Aegean Islands mentioned in the chapter.

ISLAND TAVERNA'S LAMB CHOPS

INGREDIENTS

- 4 baby lamb chops
- Kosher salt and black pepper
- ½ teaspoon rosemary
- ¼ cup parsley
- 2/3 cups Greek oil
- 1 teaspoon oregano
- 1/3 cup lemon juice

COOK TIME: 24 hours
SERVING: 1

INSTRUCTIONS

1. Place fresh lime juice in a medium mixing dish.
2. Whisk in the olive oil gradually.
3. Combine the dried rosemary, oregano, and parsley in a bowl.
4. Season with salt and pepper to taste.
5. In a resealable plastic bag, place the baby lamb chops.
6. Add half of the marinade to the bag.
7. Preheat the grill to medium-high.
8. Take the lamb chops out of the marinade.
9. Grill the chops for 3-5 minutes on each side.
10. Place on a serving dish.

GRILLED OCTUPUS WITH LEMON, OREGANO AND OLIVE OIL

INGREDIENTS

- Juice of 1 lemon
- 1 teaspoon dried oregano
- ¼ cup (60ml) olive oil
- 850g octopus

COOK TIME: 60 mins
SERVING: 4

INSTRUCTIONS

1. Combine the octopus, 1 tablespoon salt, and cold water in a large saucepan.
2. Bring the water to a boil over high heat.
3. Reduce to medium heat and cook for 50 minutes.
4. Cut tentacles when they are cool enough to handle.
5. Drizzle olive oil over everything in a big mixing bowl.
6. Season with salt and pepper to taste, then mix well to blend.
7. Preheat a chargrill that has been gently oiled to high heat.
8. Chargrill octopus for 3-5 minutes, regularly rotating, until darkened all over.
9. Drizzle with lime juice and oregano and place on a serving plate.
10. Serve right away.

ISLANDS STEAK SALAD

INGREDIENTS

- 1 tablespoon steak sauce
- 1 beef top loin steak
- **Salad**
- ½ cup feta cheese
- ¼ cup balsamic vinaigrette
- 10 pitted Greek olives
- ¼ cup red onion
- 10 cherry tomatoes
- 2/3 cup cucumber
- 4 cups salad greens
- **Mushrooms**
- 1/8 teaspoon salt
- 1/8 teaspoon pepper
- 2 tablespoons butter
- 1 tablespoon sherry
- ½ cups mushrooms

INSTRUCTIONS

1. Rub meat with steak sauce on both sides and set aside for 10 minutes.
2. Meanwhile, sauté mushrooms in butter in a small pan until golden brown.
3. Add salt, sherry, and pepper to taste.
4. Cook for around 1-2 minutes.
5. Remove from the oven and keep warm.
6. Brush the grill rack with a little coating of oil.
7. Cover and cook the meat over medium heat.
8. Allow for a 5-minute rest before slicing.
9. Divide the Salad greens between two plates.
10. Serve steaks with olives, cucumber, tomatoes, onion, and mushrooms on top.
11. Serve right away.

COOK TIME: 25 mins
SERVING: 2

AEGAN TOMATO SAUCE SPAGHETTI

INGREDIENTS

- 1½ teaspoon sea salt
- ½ teaspoon black pepper
- 5 liters water
- 45ml olive oil
- 10 sprigs oregano
- 150g parmigiano reggiano
- 1 bay leaf
- ½ teaspoon cinnamon
- 1 teaspoon sweet paprika
- ½ teaspoon chili flakes
- 800g tomatoes
- 100ml dry white wine
- 1 large yellow onion
- 2 cloves garlic
- 500g spaghetti pasta

COOK TIME: 55 mins
SERVING: 5

INSTRUCTIONS

1. Pour the oil into a pan over medium heat.
2. After a minute, add the onions and cook for another minute.
3. Then add the garlic and chili flakes and cook for a few minutes.
4. With the wine, deglaze the pan.
5. Season with salt and pepper after adding the tomatoes and water and the paprika, oregano, bay leaf, and cinnamon.
6. Stir occasionally, and if necessary, add additional water.
7. Finally, add the Parmigiano Reggiano and stir thoroughly.
8. Meanwhile, bring a big pot of water to a boil over high heat.
9. Cook the pasta according to the package directions.
10. Return the pasta to the saucepan with the sauce and toss for a minute to allow the sauce to seep into the pasta.
11. Toss everything together and serve.

ISLANDS CHICKEN SHISH KEBABS

INGREDIENTS

- 12 cherry tomatoes
- 12 fresh mushrooms
- 2 large bell peppers
- 1 large onion
- 2 pounds chicken breast
- 6 wooden skewers
- ¼ teaspoon salt
- ¼ teaspoon black pepper
- 1 teaspoon oregano
- ½ teaspoon thyme
- 2 cloves garlic
- 1 teaspoon cumin
- ¼ cup lemon juice
- ¼ cup white vinegar
- ¼ cup olive oil

COOK TIME: 2 hours
SERVING: 6

INSTRUCTIONS

1. Combine the salt, thyme, oregano, cumin, garlic, vinegar, lemon juice, olive oil, and black pepper in a mixing bowl.
2. Toss in the chicken to evenly coat it.
3. Preheat an outside grill over moderate flame and brush the grate liberally with oil.
4. Shake off any extra liquid from the chicken after removing it from the marinade.
5. Remove the leftover marinade and toss it out.
6. Using skewers, alternate threading pieces of marinated chicken with cherry tomatoes, onion, bell pepper, and mushrooms.
7. Cook the skewers on the prepared grill, regularly rotating, for about 10 minutes, or until beautifully browned on both sides and the meat no longer appears in the middle.
8. Serve immediately.

PASTELI-SESAME-HONEY CONFECTION

INGREDIENTS

- 3 cups of white sesame seeds
- 1 strip lemon peel
- 1 1/3 cups honey

COOK TIME: 3 *hours*
SERVING: 20

INSTRUCTIONS

1. Bring the honey and lemon peel to a boil in a saucepan.
2. Continuously whisk in the sesame seeds.
3. Place a piece of baking paper on a cold work surface and spread out the heated mixture thinly and evenly.
4. Allow the pasteli to cool to room temperature before using.
5. Allow at least two to three hours for chilling.
6. Cut the pasteli with parchment paper into little pieces with kitchen shears and serve.

Tip: To eat, take off the parchment paper. Keep in an airtight jar in the refrigerator.

Chapter 6: Ionian Islands Recipes

The Greek islands' cuisine is traditional Greek cuisine. Fish is more essential in certain locations than in others; on some islands, such as Sifnos, the main meal is the lowly chickpea, while on others, such as Santorini, the small yellow split pea is the staple food. The chickpea is also a national food of Rhodes, in the form of fritters spiced with cumin, a flavor rarely seen in other regional Greek recipes and likely evoking the island's role as a crossroads between East and South. The three components of the Mediterranean, grains, grapes, and olives, reign supreme in all of the islands, but Ionian cuisine is defined by its foundations. Get a taste of these delectable food from Ionian Islands.

FRIGANIA

INGREDIENTS

- 10 Greek rusks
- **Cream**
- 3 eggs
- 1 teaspoon vanilla
- 100g cornflour
- 200g sugar
- 1-liter milk
- **Syrup**
- 1 teaspoon cinnamon
- 1 lemon, peel
- 250g water
- 300g sugar
- **Whipped Cream**
- 3 tablespoons powdered sugar
- 250g heavy whipping cream
- **Garnish**
- Almonds
- Cinnamon

COOK TIME: 60 mins
SERVING: 10

INSTRUCTIONS

1. Combine all ingredients in a pot, stir well, and cook for five minutes to make the syrup.
2. Arrange the Greek rusks in a baking dish or casserole dish.
3. Pour the heated syrup over the rusks.
4. Remove the dish and set it away.
5. Whisk together the eggs, cornflour, vanilla, and sugar to make the cream.
6. Place the milk in a pot and bring to a boil.
7. Slowly pour the milk into the bowl containing the egg mixture, stirring constantly.
8. Return the cream to the pot and simmer over medium heat after mixing.
9. Pour the heated cream over the rusks.
10. Whip the cream and icing sugar together until firm peaks form.
11. Using a spatula, spread the whipped cream on the cake.
12. To serve, sprinkle with cinnamon first, then almonds.

ORANGE-CURRANT SCONES

INGREDIENTS

- 2 large eggs beaten
- 2 tablespoons brown sugar
- 1 cup heavy cream
- 1 cup currants
- ¼ pound unsalted butter
- 1 large egg
- 1 tablespoon baking powder
- Freshly grated zest
- 2 tablespoons sugar
- 3 cups all-purpose flour

INSTRUCTIONS

1. Preheat oven to 375 degrees Fahrenheit.
2. In a large mixing bowl, combine the dry ingredients and zest.
3. Rub the butter and flour mixture together with your hands or a pastry cutter.
4. Make a well in the center of the bowl and pour in the egg and cream.
5. Hand-mix the ingredients until a shaggy dough is produced.
6. Cut the large rectangle into eight or twelve smaller rectangles.
7. Place them evenly spaced on the baking sheet.
8. Top with an egg wash and a dusting of brown sugar.
9. Bake for 22 minutes, or until light golden brown.
10. Warm or at room temperature is OK.
11. Within 24 hours, eat.

COOK TIME: 30 mins
SERVING: 8

TUNISIAN TOMATO SOUP WITH CHICKPEA

INGREDIENTS

- 1 (28 ounces) can of tomatoes
- 2 cups cooked chickpeas
- 2 teaspoons cumin
- 3 bay leaves
- 1 teaspoon turmeric
- 1 ½ teaspoon cumin seeds
- 2 tablespoons garlic
- 2 teaspoons salt
- 1 tablespoon olive oil
- 3 cups onions
- 1 cinnamon stick
- 7 cups water
- 1 cup lentils
- **Optional**
- Parsley, chopped
- Fresh mint
- Currants
- Plain yogurt
- Cayenne pepper
- Black pepper

COOK TIME: 75 mins
SERVING: 6

INSTRUCTIONS

1. Bring Seven cups of water to a boil with the lentils and cinnamon stick in a large soup pot.
2. Reduce heat to low and simmer for half an hour, or until soft vegetables.
3. In the meantime, heat the oil in a soup pot.
4. Add the garlic, onion, bay leaves, ground cumin, cumin seeds, turmeric, salt, and turmeric.
5. Cook for 5 to 10 minutes over medium heat.
6. Bring the mashed tomatoes and liquid from the can to a boil.
7. Reduce to low heat and cook for another fifteen minutes, slightly covered.
8. Cook for 5 minutes after adding the chickpeas and lentils.
9. Season with the two peppers and lemon juice and salt to taste.
10. Serve with a dollop of yogurt on the side.

TSIGARELI

INGREDIENTS

- 1 ¼ cups fresh dill
- Salt and hot paprika
- 2 garlic cloves
- ¼ cup tomato paste
- 2 large onions
- 1 large fennel bulb
- ¼ cup olive oil
- 2 ½ pounds tender greens

COOK TIME: 30 mins
SERVING: 4

INSTRUCTIONS

1. In a big saucepan or wok, heat 2 tablespoons of olive oil.
2. Covered and over low heat, simmer the greens in the oil.
3. In a large pan, heat the olive oil and sauté the onions, occasionally turning, until tender, about 5-8 minutes.
4. Cook the fennel bulb in the same pan as the onions.
5. Stir in the tomato paste and garlic for about 60 seconds.
6. Simmer over low heat with the wilted greens.
7. Stir it in about five minutes after adding the dill.
8. Season with salt and sweet or spicy paprika to taste.
9. Drizzle a little extra virgin olive oil over the greens.

RABBIT STEWED IN TOMATO AND RED WINE

INGREDIENTS

- Steamed rice to serve
- 1 cup white wine
- Sea salt
- Black pepper
- 1 cinnamon stick
- 1.5-liter hot water
- ¼ teaspoon nutmeg
- 4 whole cloves
- 1 teaspoon sugar
- 2 bay leaves
- 1 cup red wine
- 1 ½ cups puréed tomato
- 1 medium red onion
- 4 cloves garlic
- 1/3 cup olive oil
- 1 kg golden shallots
- 1 x 1.5 kg rabbit

COOK TIME: 60 mins
SERVING: 6

INSTRUCTIONS

1. Whisk together the wine and vinegar to make the marinade.
2. Place the rabbit pieces in a bowl and pour the marinade over them.
3. In a heavy-bottomed frying pan, heat the olive oil over medium heat.
4. Sauté shallots until golden.
5. Sauté red onion and garlic in the same oil until transparent.
6. Drain the rabbit pieces and lightly brown them on all sides.
7. Simmer until the liquid is evaporated, then add the wine.
8. Combine the cinnamon stick, cloves, nutmeg, bay leaves, sugar, tomato, and half of the boiling water in a large mixing bowl.
9. Cook for another half an hour after adding the cooked shallots.
10. Remove the bay leaves and cloves before seasoning and serve with steaming rice.

ISLAND SOFRITO

INGREDIENTS

- 6 fresh tomatillos
- 1 cup chopped garlic
- 1 bunch green onions
- 1 ½ cup cilantro leaves
- 1 yellow bell pepper
- 10 tomatoes
- 2 red bell peppers
- 1 orange bell pepper

COOK TIME: 45 mins
SERVING: 12

INSTRUCTIONS

1. Combine the orange, red, green, and yellow bell peppers in a blender.
2. Combine the tomatillos, cilantro, green onions, tomatoes, and garlic in a large mixing bowl.
3. Depending on your choice, you can blend or pulse the ingredients.
4. Keep refrigerated in an airtight container.

Tip: Refrigerate the sofrito in resealable bags for later use, or spoon into ice cube pans to freeze in parts.

Conclusion

Greek cuisine provides a vast and varied selection of dishes and drinks resulting from thousands of years of living, preparing, and eating. Each Greek dinner is both fresh and appealing, as well as a reflection to Greece's history. Until the Middle Ages, many of the ingredients utilized in current Greek food were unknown. The use of potatoes, tomatoes, spinach, bananas, and other fruits and vegetables in preparing food has been adopted from American food culture. Greek cuisine is simple and elegant, with subtle to powerful tastes, smooth to crunchy textures, and an ageless freshness. Preparing and eating Greek food is an exciting excursion into the cradle of civilization and the home of the Gods of Olympus, no matter where you are on the globe. One of the delights we can all share is the discovering, tasting, and experiencing Greek cuisine.

Printed in Great Britain
by Amazon

11164963R00115